A Brief View
of the Constitution
of the United States

Da Capo Press Reprints in

AMERICAN CONSTITUTIONAL AND LEGAL HISTORY

GENERAL EDITOR: LEONARD W. LEVY

Claremont Graduate School

A Brief View
of the Constitution
of the United States
Addressed to the Law Academy of Philadelphia

by Peter S. Du Ponceau, L.L.D.

DA CAPO PRESS • NEW YORK • 1974

Library of Congress Cataloging in Publication Data

Du Ponceau, Peter Stephen, 1760-1844.
    A brief view of the Constitution of the United
States, addressed to the Law Academy of Philadelphia.

    (Da Capo Press reprints in American constitutional
and legal history)
    Reprint of the ed. published by E. G. Dorsey,
Philadelphia.
    1. United States — Constitutional law. I. Title.
KF4550.Z9D87   1974   342'.73'02   72-124893
ISBN 0-306-71986-X

This Da Capo Press edition of *A Brief View of the Constitution of the United States* is an unabridged republication of
the 1834 edition published in Philadelphia. It is reprinted
with permission from a copy in the Columbia University
Libraries.

Published by Da Capo Press, Inc.
A Subsidiary of Plenum Publishing Corporation
227 West 17th Street, New York, N.Y. 10011

A BRIEF VIEW

OF THE

CONSTITUTION OF THE UNITED STATES.

A

BRIEF VIEW

OF THE

Constitution of the United States,

ADDRESSED

TO THE

LAW ACADEMY OF PHILADELPHIA.

BY PETER S. DU PONCEAU, LL.D.
Provost of the Academy.

PUBLISHED BY AND FOR THE ACADEMY.

PHILADELPHIA:
E. G. DORSEY, PRINTER, 16 LIBRARY STREET.
....
1834

CONTENTS.

CHAPTER III.

Organization of the Government.

SECTION 1.

SECTION 2

SECTION 3.

PREFACE.

———

THIS little work has no pretensions, save that of brevity and clearness. It is intended for the benefit of youth, of the general reader, and of foreigners. I believe that no attempt of the kind has yet been made; I mean on so limited a scale. I have endeavoured by a method of my own, to compress in plain and popular language, the prominent features of our excellent constitution in as small a space as possible, and at the same time to avoid obscurity. Whether I have succeeded or not, it is for the reader to determine.

I have addressed this essay (for it claims no higher title) to the *Law Academy of Philadelphia*. For more than fourteen years I have had the honour of being at the head of that useful institution, who, during that time have been zealously pursuing their steady course, and whose members have enriched the legal profession with several valuable works. It is not so much for their instruction that I have presented them with this result of my studies, as that they might see in it a tribute of friendship and a testimony of my constant attachment, and of the pleasure that I feel in being connected with them. Yet I have thought that this brief view of our constitution might not be useless to their younger members, as an introduction to the more elaborate works which they will be called upon to study. It will smooth their way to a more profound investigation of the rules and principles of our admirable form of government.

The method which I have followed to attain the object which I had in view, is, I believe, entirely new. I do not by any means pretend that it is preferable to that which has been adopted by other writers; I only can say that I found it better suited to my purpose, which I have already explained. Had I written with other and more ambitious views, I would, of course, have endeavoured to adapt my method to them, as our great writers on the constitution have very properly and successfully done.

I have treated separately and in the first place, of the *organization* of the government, by which I mean its great division into legislative, executive and judicial departments; its consequent subdivisions; its subordinate officers; the various modes of election and appointment to office; the periods of service; the modes of action of those different authorities, and a variety of matter of detail, constituting together what might be called the *mechanical* part of the government. In the text of the constitution those matters are mixed with other provisions; I have thought best to present them in a separate view.

These being disposed of, I have proceeded to the enumeration and distribution of powers, rights and duties between the general government and the states, *reddendo singula singulis*, and so as to give a clear view not only of the division of power between the union and the individual states, but of its distribution between the different branches which compose the aggregate authority of the former. I have classed these under general heads, with reference to the different subjects on which power is or may be exercised; in which division or classification I have followed no precedent, because I found none which, in my opinion, could so well answer my purpose as the arrangement which I have adopted. By this means I have been enabled to condense a great deal more matter in a small space than I could otherwise have done. I have even been able to introduce a few occasional reflections, and to deduce a few corollaries from the text of the constitution, which do not appear on the face of the instrument. But of these I have been very sparing; and the reader will recollect that it is not an abstract, but a *view* of the constitution that I here present to the public, and consequently, that where the text, in consequence of different opinions having been entertained about its meaning, appeared to require some explanation, it be-

2

hoved me to give that which appeared to me to be
most consonant to its spirit.

I have prefaced the whole work with two prelimi-
nary chapters, in one of which I have endeavoured to
give a clear view of the political state of this country under
the colonial government and under the confederation,
with which in the other chapter I have compared our
present constitution, in order to facilitate its intelli-
gence, by pointing out the objects that its framers had
in view. In an appendix, I have given the text of the
Constitution, with its amendments, and the Articles of
Confederation and Perpetual Union, which preceded it.
To these I have added the Declaration of Independence, and the Farewell Address of our immortal
Washington, considering them as indispensable docu-
ments to the student of our constitution, and of our
constitutional history.

I have not included in this short sketch much of
what is called *constitutional law*. It is a separate science, depending on acts of legislation, which may be
altered from day to day. Even the decisions of the
supreme court of the United States, on constitutional
points, have been questioned, after being acquiesced in
for many years. I have, in a few instances, touched on
some of those questions; the whole subject, however, I
have not considered to be within my plan. *A brief
view* of the constitution could not admit of it.

I have considered the constitution and its amendments as one instrument, and therefore I have not generally distinguished the provisions of the former from
those of the latter. A reference to the text will show
the sources whence my positions are derived. The
student should make himself familiar with it. This
work is only intended to facilitate its study, and to give
a general view of it to those who do not wish to go far-
ther. I believe that the text and the works of its able
commentators, will be studied with more ease after
reading this little tract than they would be without it.

I have, as much as possible, used the words and
phraseology of the constitution in stating its contents;
but the reader will easily perceive that it was not always in my power so to do consistently with the arrangement which I have adopted. But I have never
knowingly, at least, varied from the exact sense.

Such is the plan I have pursued, and which I submit to the candour and indulgence of my readers.

Having thus explained the design of this essay, and
the method which I have followed, I hope I shall be
excused, if I subjoin a few reflections, which an atten-
tive study of our constitution and forty-five years' experience under it, have suggested to me. It will be
remembered that I write principally for youth, that
they may be enabled, when they grow up to manhood,

to avoid the errors which experience has shown us to
be the most dangerous to the permanency of our Union.

The *duration of empires* has been considered by states-
men and patriots in all countries and in all ages, as the
most important object to which the policy of nations
should be directed. *Esto perpetua,* was the last fervent
wish of the excellent Father Paul, on behalf of his beloved Venice. It was also the last wish of our illustrious Washington. It breathes through every line of
his admirable Farewell Address to the people of the
United States. Therefore, the first and last wish of
every good citizen, is or ought to be *the perpetuity of
our Union.* It has not yet lasted *half a century;* and
during that short period, it has sustained many shocks
that have endangered its existence. Those dangers
have been surmounted by the good sense and the virtue of the people; but the political, like the natural
body, is not immortal, and it will sink at last, if efficient means are not taken to prevent the recurrence
of those disorders, which gradually weaken it, and
must at last operate its dissolution.

The cause of those disorders is chiefly to be traced
to the too great prevalence of party spirit. I admit
that parties, when kept within moderate bounds, are a
wholesome ingredient in a free community; but they
are a deadly poison, when carried to excess; particularly when they are not so much founded on the difference of political opinions, as on a blind attachment
to popular leaders. The Roman republic was near

her fall, when parties came to be distinguished by the names of Sylla and Marius, and of Cæsar and Pompey. Those leaders usurped all the power, and were followed by a succession of tyrants. In the bright days of our commonwealth, we never heard of Washington-men, nor of Adams, Jefferson or Madison-men. The true republican citizen is neither of Paul nor of Apollos;* he is no man's man; he is his cou..try's man and his own man. No man, however great or illustrious, should be identified with virtues or with principles. It leads in religion to idolatry, and in politics to submission to despotism.

Among the evil consequences which follow from party spirit carried to excess, is a lamentable fluctuation in the maxims and policy of the government. These suddenly change, as one party obtains the ascendancy over the other, and foreigners, as well as citizens, do not know any more what to rely on. The decrees of legislative assemblies, the decisions of supreme tribunals, a long acquiescence in those decrees and decisions; all those things are set at nought to serve the views of party leaders. The country must be again agitated with questions which were believed to be at rest, to be agitated again when the opposite party shall have acquired the supremacy. It is impossible, that amidst such frequent changes, a country should long continue to be happy at home and respectable abroad.

* 1 Cor. 1. xii.

2 *

The mischievous effects of a mutable policy in a republic, are well depicted in the 62d number of the Federalist. "Those," says the eloquent writer, "would fill a volume. It forfeits the respect and confidence of other nations, lays us open to their intrigues, and make us a prey to those who have an interest in speculating on our fluctuating councils and embarrassed affairs. At home it destroys confidence in our government, kills the spirit of enterprise, which no longer knows on what to rely; and what is most deplorable is that diminution of reverence and attachment which steals into the hearts of the people, towards a political system which betrays so many marks of infirmity, and disappoints so many of their flattering hopes. No government, any more than an individual, will be long respected, without being truly respectable, nor be truly respectable without order and stability."

I have abridged this admirable passage, and recommend to the reader to turn to the original, which will well repay his trouble. I regret to be obliged to say that we have experienced more than once this fluctuation of policy, and that at this moment we are again in danger of suffering from its baneful effects. Questions have been and are still agitated that make us tremble for the stability of our institutions.

Standing as I do, unconnected with any party, I have not hesitated, when occasion has offered, to express my opinion freely on some of those points. On one particularly, the renewed discussion of which, after a long acquiescence, agitates the country from one end to the other, I have thought it my duty, as a constitutional writer, to be clear and explicit. I allude to the subject of a National Bank. Its constitutionality I have long considered as settled by the competent authorities, and acquiesced in by the people at large; of its expediency I am fully convinced. I consider it necessary under our form of government not only to regulate the currency, chiefly consisting of bills of credit, issued under the authority of twenty-four different states, but also to preserve a due equality among those states. As the subject, to my knowledge, has not yet been presented in this last point of view, I hope I shall be excused if I explain myself somewhat more at large upon it.

One of the objects of our constitution is to maintain equality among the states, as that of the state constitutions is to preserve it among the individuals that compose them. With this view, no doubt, the senate has been established, and republican forms of government are mutually guaranteed. The principle of equality which these imply is not less necessary among United or confederated states than among individual citizens. These United States are advancing in power and riches to an astonishing, but not in an equal degree. The constitution was intended to be so organized that no

single state and no combination of states should acquire
an undue ascendancy over the rest. There is a tendency to that effect in all confederated states. It is well
known that, in former times, Holland possessed such an
ascendancy in the confederation of the United Nether-
lands, and the Canton of Berne in that of Switzerland. At
this day Austria predominates in confederated Germany,
and her will is the law of the less powerful states; the
struggles of Athens and Sparta for the supremacy over
the republics of Greece, and the bloody wars to which
they gave rise, can never be forgotten. The same danger threatens us unless ambitious states are prevented
from rising above the others. Our states are, with few
exceptions, nearly equal in territory; but there is a
great difference in their means of acquiring riches, and
that difference arises from certain natural advantages.
Riches give influence and influence leads to power.
The means by which it may be acquired are sufficiently obvious. Money is the great engine by which such
a purpose is usually effected, and there is no knowing
what might not be done by a monied institution, with
a large capital, wielded by a great, rich and ambitious
state. The bank of Amsterdam did not contribute a
little to the ascendancy of Holland over the states of
the Dutch Union. A State Bank may produce the
same effect among us, unless it be checked by the
financial power of the nation. In what form, or under
what modifications and restrictions a National Bank
should be established to prevent its becoming danger-

ous to the creating power or to the country, it is not my business to consider. A wise and prudent legislation is all that is required for that purpose.

I have, in like manner, ventured to express my opinion on some minor points, and have abstained from the consideration of others. I have said nothing on the questions which have been lately stirred, and which happily appear now to be at rest. I have not inquired whether a state can secede from the Union, or of its own authority declare an act of congress null and void. I feared lest the shade of Washington should frown upon me.*

Neither have I said anything respecting the question so often agitated, whether the constitution should be construed strictly or liberally? All I have to say on this subject is that I think it should be construed *fairly* and *honestly*, always keeping in view the objects for which it was made.

On a general view of the instrument and a retrospection of the events that have taken place since it has been in operation, I have come to the conclusion, that there is no danger of our Union's degenerating into a consolidated government over this extensive country, and consequently of its destroying the exist-

* See Washington's Farewell Address in the Appendix.

ence of the states, as independent communities within the limits to them prescribed; there is much more danger, on the contrary, of a dissolution of that admirable Union, the pride of our land and the envy of all the world besides. The organization of the general government, and the powers which the states have reserved to themselves, are not only sufficient to secure the independent existence of the latter, but recent events have shown that they are even possessed of the means to make themselves formidable to those who might attempt to encroach upon their constitutional rights. What has been done by a single state, when nothing more than a doubtful local interest was in question, shows what might be done by a combination of states, if more serious disturbances should take place.

I have shown in this essay, that the general government cannot be conveniently administered in all its details, without the aid of the state authorities. This I have called the *auxiliary system*, which is one of the foundations on which our Union rests. Take that foundation away, and the whole machine will be disorganized. An attempt on the part of congress to exercise all its powers by means of its own officers, spread like locusts in swarms through our land, would unavoidably fail. Its security depends on its being formidable abroad, strong and respected at home, but felt as little as possible by the individual citizens. The moment it shall attempt to grasp at more, a dissolution of the

Union will be at hand. It is, no doubt, under this impression that congress have confided to the state courts the power of naturalization and other judicial powers, that they have avoided laying direct taxes, except in cases of great necessity, and in collecting them the state assessments have been generally adopted as a basis of computation. An excise law once produced an insurrection in Pennsylvania; the like has not been attempted ever since. These powers, undoubtedly, are vested in the national government; but not to be rashly or wantonly used. Upon the whole, a mutual dependence exists between the Union and the states, without which the former cannot be preserved. When differences have arisen between the general and the state governments, conciliation has been found the most effectual means of settling them. The constitution itself is the result of compromise, and is best preserved by the same means by which it has been obtained. May heaven avert for many ages, the fatal period when our differences shall have to be settled by brutal force! Between powers so nicely balanced, a collision is ever to be dreaded.

An intelligent foreigner, after perusing these sheets, made the following remark: "Your constitution was made for a *virtuous people;* but it will not suit any other." Let us, then, continue to be virtuous, and we may hope to be long united, happy and free

With these few observations, I submit this little work to the impartial public. I have endeavoured to give a view of the constitution as I understand it, without regard to party opinions, and much less to party interests: these are transient; but truth and reason are eternal. I have written for the rising generation; I have spoken to them the language which I firmly believe they or their descendants will one day hear from posterity.

A

BRIEF VIEW

OF THE

Constitution of the United States.

CHAPTER I.

PRELIMINARY OBSERVATIONS.

SECTION 1.—*State of the Colonies before and during the Revolution.*

BEFORE the revolution the British colonies in America were independent of each other, but separately dependent on the king, and in some measure on the parliament of Great Britain. The extent of that dependence was not accurately defined; its general principles were, however, sufficiently understood, so that, at least ever since the final expulsion of the Stuarts from the throne of Great Britain, in 1688, the mother country and the colonies went on harmoniously together, without any but trifling differences, which did not interrupt

A

their union. It was understood that in return for the
protection which the former afforded to the latter, particularly against their neighbours, the French, who,
until a few years before the revolution, were in posses-
sion of Canada, and also against the Indians in alliance
with them, she had a right to monopolize their commerce, and with that view, to restrict it by laws and
regulations. The crown also interfered in various ways
in their internal government, which was, in general,
modelled upon that of Great Britain, though the forms
differed in several particulars, which did not, however, affect the substantial principles of the British constitution, to which they all clung with enthusiastic
affection; and, of course, their governments, though dif-
fering in some details, were all founded on the representative combined with the monarchical principle.
Trial by jury, in civil as well as in criminal cases, the
writ of habeas corpus. and the liberty of the press, were
among the privileges which they most cherished, and
were incorporated in all their codes. Thus they
enjoyed as much civil and political liberty as could
come to the share of dependent states; and, above
all, the precious right of not being obliged to part
with their money, but by their free will and consent;
without which, colour it as you will, every form of government, however free or republican in its outward
appearance, is but slavery in disguise. Otherwise, the
crown of England possessed great power and influence
in their separate governments. In most of the colo-

nics, the executive branch was dependent upon it; the governors being appointed by the king; and the judges, as well as many other officers, held their offices mediately or immediately under him. The crown, moreover, had a negative on all the laws passed by the colonial legislature, which it exercised through its governors or through the council of state. So that, on the whole, the mother country possessed powers sufficient to enforce her colonial system, and keep her American possessions in check, while these were left at liberty to regulate their internal affairs in the manner best suited to their peculiar situation, and to promote among themselves all the arts, that did not interfere with the interests or policy of Great Britain.

In this situation the British colonies prospered beyond any other of the European settlements in America. They were happy and contented. They were proud of being constituent parts of a great empire; they gloried in the name of English subjects, and never would have thought (at least for a long time) of changing their condition, if the parliament of Great Britain, in an evil hour, had not formed and avowed the project of reducing them to an absolute subjection to their power.

We have said above that no freedom can exist, where the people can be compelled to part with their money, without their consent, or that of their representatives. The people of the colonies were not represented in the

British parliament; therefore, it was evident that that body had no right to impose upon them taxes of any kind, unless they were absolutely necessary for the regulation of their commerce. The practice had been, when the mother country wanted funds for some objects in which the colonies were interested, to apply for aid to their respective legislatures, which they, in general, freely granted. But scarcely had Great Britain, with the assistance of those colonies, made the conquest of Canada, and compelled France and Spain to submit to humiliating treaties, that there were no bounds to her ambition; and she began to look on her colonies as sources from whence she might draw money at her pleasure. Intoxicated with success, she not only claimed the right of taxing them without any limitation; but, as if that were not sufficient, she also claimed that of binding them by her statutes *in all cases what-soever.* This was slavery without disguise. Yet the colonies might have suffered the parent state to enjoy her theories, if she had not attempted to carry them into practice, and to enforce their execution by her arms. The means that she took for that purpose, and the resistance that was made, are within the province of history. Suffice it to say, that in consequence of these, serious differences arose, and a civil war, at last, was kindled between the colonies and the mother country, which resulted in the separation of thirteen of those colonies, and their declaring themselves free and independent states.

This declaration, as every one knows, took place on the memorable 4th of July, 1776. At that moment, and by virtue of that solemn act, each of these colonies became a free, sovereign, and independent state; each became free to act as it should think proper; sovereign within its limits, and independent of the whole world besides.

A union, however, subsisted between them at the time of this declaration. A congress had been assembled at Philadelphia, towards the end of the year 1774, consisting of delegates from the different colonies, who had no powers given to them, but to consult and advise on the best means of obtaining the redress of their grievances from Great Britain, and restoring harmony with the mother country. When this plan was adopted, hopes of a reconciliation were still entertained. Consequently the first congress confined themselves to sending humble petitions to the British king and parliament, and spirited addresses to their fellow-subjects in the various parts of the empire. To these and some recommendations to the people of the colonies, which were punctually obeyed, the proceedings of this congress were confined; and after a short session, they separated.

A second congress was convened to meet at the same place on the 10th of May, 1775, invested with no greater powers than the former. When this new assembly met, the face of affairs had considerably changed.

2 A

Hostilities had begun between the mother country and the colonies. The battle of Lexington had been fought on the 19th of April preceding, and every thing announced an impending war between the two countries. Great Britain declared her intention to compel the colonies to submit by force of arms, and that determination soon brought on actual war. Congress, supported by the confidence of the people, but without any express powers, undertook to direct the storm, and were seconded by the people and by the colonial authorities. They issued paper money, raised troops by requisitions, appointed officers, settled their pay and emoluments, directed military operations, and in little more than a year after their meeting, they proclaimed independence, without making any other change in the state of things. It was not until the 15th of November 1777, that they presented to the new states for their acceptance articles of confederation and perpetual union, which were not adopted by all until the year 1781, when Maryland was the last that ratified them.

In the mean time congress went on as if they had been invested with the most explicit powers; they went even so far as to bind the nation by treaties with France, by one of which they guaranteed all the possessions of that kingdom in the West Indies. It was not, as far as we know, even thought necessary that those treaties should be ratified by the state legislatures. No one, at that time, denied the *constitutionality* of those powers, which congress exercised for the defence of the country, and the general welfare, though they had no other authority to show for them than the tacit consent of the people; and it is remarkable that in none of the constitutions that were made in the years 1776 and 1777, after the Declaration of Independence, and before the articles of confederation were submitted to the states, among which constitutions may be mentioned those of New York, Pennsylvania, Maryland, and North Carolina, nothing was said of the treaty-making power, or of that of declaring war and making peace, so well was it understood that those powers did not belong to the individual states, but to the *United States*, under whatever form their general government might thereafter be constituted. *The union* was deeply rooted, and had its most solid foundations in the hearts of the people, who gloried in being not a cluster of independent communities, but a great, respectable, and powerful *nation*.

This undefined state of things ceased on the 12th of February, 1781, when by the accession of Maryland, the articles of confederation and perpetual union became the national law of the whole thirteen states. They were very inadequate to what the critical situation of the country required; but the people's minds were not yet prepared for a more comprehensive and more efficient form of government.

SECT. 2.—*Of the Articles of Confederation and Perpetual Union.*

This celebrated compact began with a declaration that each state retained its sovereignty, freedom and independence, and every power, jurisdiction and right, which the confederation did not expressly delegate to the United States in congress assembled. It proceeded to define the confederation itself to be a league of friendship between the states for their common defence, the security of their liberties, and their mutual and general welfare; and lastly the states bound themselves, in their sovereign and independent capacities, to assist each other against all external force. To promote good neighbourhood between the confederates, the free inhabitants of each state, (paupers and vagabonds only excepted,) were to be entitled to the privileges of citizens in all the others; fugitives from justice were to be mutually delivered up, and full faith and credit were to be given in each of the states, to the records, acts, and judicial proceedings of the others. It is not a little remarkable that no provision was made for the delivering up of fugitive slaves, which seems to have been left entirely to the good faith of the states.

The formation of the congress was established on the principle of the sovereignty and independence of the states. Its members were in fact no more than ambassadors, under the name of *delegates*, (*legati*,) from

the states which sent them. Each state was to send a
number of such delegates, not less than two, nor more
than seven; to maintain them at its own expense, and
to recall them at pleasure, even within the year for
which they were appointed.

To this congress was given a splendid array of powers, which in appearance placed them on a line with
the most potent sovereigns of the earth; but it was in
appearance only, for the substance was denied them,
the states having reserved to themselves all the means
of carrying those powers into execution. Thus congress
might declare and carry on war, make treaties of
peace, alliance and commerce, decree the raising of
land forces, and the quotas of each state, build and fit
out ships of war, borrow money and issue bills of credit
on the faith of the nation; but none of those powers
could be exercised without the co-operation of the individual states: if an army was to be raised, all that congress could do, was to make requisitions to the states
for their respective quotas of men in arms; and it was
the same when money was wanted, as congress had no
power to raise it directly or indirectly in the shape of
taxes. The states, it is true, were expressly bound by
the articles of confederation to furnish those quotas when
required; the mode of assessment was also fixed by that
instrument; it was in proportion to the value of all
land within each state granted to or surveyed for any
person, with the buildings and improvements thereon,

as the same should be estimated in such manner as congress might from time to time prescribe. But congress had no power to compel the states to fulfil those engagements; the moral bond was all they had to rely upon, and every one knows how weak is that tie upon states as well as upon individuals, if not strengthened by a power, which they cannot resist, and which they are forced to obey. To increase the difficulty, congress could not exercise the powers which we have enumerated without the concurrence of the delegates of more than two-thirds of the states, that is to say, of nine out of thirteen. The votes were taken by states, represented by their delegates. If the members of a delegation were equally divided in opinion on a particular point, it followed that the state that they represented, was so far deprived of a voice, which still increased the difficulty of obtaining the required majority.

The states, it is true, were prohibited from separately exercising the powers which they had conferred on the congress; they could not, without the consent of that body, send or receive embassies, or make treaties with foreign governments; neither could they, without such consent, engage in war, unless in case of actual invasion, or of imminent danger of being attacked by the Indians. They could not grant commissions to ships of war, or issue letters of marque or reprisal, except after a declaration of war by congress, or in case of their being infested by pirates, and then only until congress

should determine otherwise; nor could they keep on
foot any body of forces in time of peace, except such
as congress should think necessary for garrisoning their
forts; and in order to prevent their confederating with
each other, to the detriment of the union, no two or
more states were to enter into any treaty, confederation or alliance whatever with each other, without the
consent of the United States in congress assembled. But
those prohibitions, while they paralyzed the action of
the states, added no strength to that of the union, which
still was dependent on the precarious compliance of
each individual state with the requisitions of the federal
head.

As congress had no power to levy taxes or imposts
of any kind, the regulation of commerce remained entirely with the individual states. Each state might act
in that respect as it thought proper; and therefore the
nation, as such, could not countervail the fiscal regulations of foreign powers, however much they might tend
to the detriment of the agriculture, commerce or manufactures of the country; while, on the other hand, it was
lawful for the states to carry on a war of commercial
regulations against each other, which would inevitably
have resulted in a dissolution of the union, and perhaps
at last in bloody hostilities between its members.

Such were the most prominent features of that confederation, which, as it were by a miracle, carried the

United States through the "war of independence." A few years of peace made its imperfections manifest to all; and in the year 1787, a convention of delegates from all the states met at Philadelphia, in order to remedy its defects. The result of their labours was the present *constitution of the United States.*

CHAPTER II.

THE title of this instrument at once points out the difference between it and the *confederation* that existed before. It bears on its face the stamp of a national government; and it was, no doubt, the view of the framers to give that character to the new compact that was about to be entered into, without, however, infringing on the sovereignty of the states more than was absolutely necessary to attain the objects declared in the instrument, and those were expressed to be "to form a more perfect union; to establish justice, insure domestic tranquillity, provide for the common defence, promote the general welfare, and secure for ever the blessings of liberty."

This was a most difficult task to be accomplished. A confederation, in the strict sense of the word, had been attempted and had failed; a consolidation of the states under one general government, of which they should be mere subordinate districts or provinces, was not even thought of, it being well understood that such a government could not exist over such a widely extended coun

B

try under republican forms, and that it would inevitably lead to a monarchy, and perhaps to despotism. A form of government therefore was resolved upon, which should be compounded of both, in such a manner as not to deprive the states of more of their sovereignty and independence, than was necessary to insure the permanency of the union and the welfare and safety of the whole.

To designate this new form of government, the word *constitution* was substituted to that of *confederation*, while on the other hand the denomination of *United States* was retained, the former being expressive of a *national*, the latter of a *federal* system. The purely federal clauses by which, in the articles of confederation, the states are said to retain their "sovereignty, freedom and independence," "to be bound to each other in a firm league of friendship, and to bind themselves to assist each other against foreign aggression," were left out of the new compact, as inconsistent with its spirit, and what remained of sovereignty in the states after the concessions made to the government of the union, was left, as a matter of inference, to be gathered from the context of the whole instrument, in which the word "sovereignty" is not once used, as applied to the states. And in order to stamp the national character upon it from the very outset, the preamble begins with these remarkable words. "We, the *people* of the United States . . . , . . . do ordain and establish this *constitution* for the

United States of America." Thus excluding the idea of a mere confederation of independent communities, by making the people at large a party to this compact, and binding not only each state, but every individual to each other, and to the government of their creation. In these terms the constitution was afterwards ratified by the people of the states, assembled in conventions for that purpose. After its adoption, however, it received some amendments, made in one of the forms which the constitution prescribes. By one of those amendments, it is provided, that "the enumeration, in the constitution, of certain rights, shall not be construed to deny or disparage others, retained by the people;" and by another, that "the powers not delegated to the United States by the constitution, nor prohibited by it to the states, are reserved to the states respectively, or to the people." This last clause was borrowed from the articles of confederation; but is less strongly expressed.

That there are strong federal features in this instrument is not to be denied; but upon the whole, the national character is predominant, as will be seen from the distribution of the powers mutually conceded and reserved.

Among the powers with which the rulers of mankind are or may be invested, are those which writers on public law have denominated, by way of preeminence, *jura summi imperii*, that is to say, the rights of sove-

reignty in the highest degree." Such are principally
the rights or powers to make war and conclude peace,
to enter into treaties of alliance and commerce, to send
and receive ambassadors, to coin money, fix the standard of weights and measures, raise and equip fleets
and armies, borrow money on the credit of the nation,
and others of a similar nature.

Most of these powers were conferred, by the articles of confederation, on the congress of the United
States; but it was in the power of any one of the
states to withhold its share of the means for carrying
them into execution. The congress therefore possessed
the pageantry, the mere name of sovereignty, not sovereignty itself. It was the agent of thirteen sovereigns that might at any time defeat its measures, by
refusing or neglecting to comply with its requisitions.

The framers of the present constitution found, of
course, no difficulty in conferring on the new government the same powers that had been given, by the articles of confederation, to the congress of the United
States, and they freely granted them in the same exclusive manner; but it was necessary, at the same
time, to grant the means to execute them independently of the governments of the states; and that could
not be done without putting into the hands of the national authorities the two great engines of national
sovereignty, the *purse* and the *sword*. The convention

magnanimously agreed to this surrender. The congress was empowered to lay taxes, and to raise and maintain fleets and armies, with their own means, under trifling restrictions, which will be mentioned in their proper places.

It was not enough to give to the general government the use and the direction of the *military* sword, it was necessary also to place in their hands the sword *of justice*, at least as far as was necessary to enable them by its means, to give effect to the laws that they are authorized to make, and this was done in the manner that we shall presently show.

Thus far we have seen how the framers of our constitution, at the same time that they continued in the general government the *jura summi imperii*, which had been vested in the old congress, furnished it with ample means to carry those powers into execution. But this valuable instrument contains many important details, which may, in a great measure, be considered as corollaries of the great principle on which the convention acted, and of which we have shown the most prominent features.

It cannot have escaped the observation of the reader, that the powers now vested in the general government, could not be confided to a single body, such as was the former congress; here was no longer a confederation, but

B 2

a national government, acting, within certain limits, independently of the states, upon all and every one of the individuals of which they were composed, and armed with compulsory means to enforce obedience to its decrees; it was therefore indispensably necessary to divide those ample powers, so as to guard in the best possible manner against their abuse. Therefore the new government was established on the model of those of the states, with legislative, executive, and judicial departments, distinct and separate from each other. We shall now give a succinct view of its organization, and of the distribution of the powers granted among the several branches of the national government, showing at the same time, what powers are reserved to the states in their separate capacity, and upon the whole in what manner the state and the national authorities are balanced and made to harmonize with each other.

CHAPTER III.

ORGANIZATION OF THE GOVERNMENT.

Section 1.—*Of the Legislative Department.*

The legislature is composed of two branches, a senate and a house of representatives.

The senate represents the states in their federative capacities. Its members are elected for six years by the state legislatures; one-third of them go out every second year. Each state has two senators. When assembled, however, they vote individually and not by states; so that a state that has but one senator present, has in fact but half a vote.

The representatives are elected in each state by the people at large. Their numbers are in proportion to the population of the state which sends them; in states where there are slaves, three-fifths of them are included in the computation of their population; Indians, not taxed, are excluded every where. The number of representatives is not to exceed one for every thirty thousand; but each state is at least to have one. The representatives are elected for two years. Every ten years a census, or enumeration of the inhabitants, is to be made; upon which congress determine by a law the number of representatives that each state is to send. The first of these enumerations was made in 1790, the last in 1830.

The times, places, and manner of holding elections for senators and representatives are prescribed by the legislature of each state; but congress may by law make or alter such regulations, except as to places for choosing senators. This, however, they have not yet done, but left it to the states, who elect senators by joint or separate ballots of the two houses of their legislatures, and representatives by popular election. The electors of the latter must be qualified to elect members of the most numerous branch of the legislature of their state.

The requisite qualifications for a senator are, to be 30 years of age, to have been nine years a citizen of the United States; to be a representative requires only 25 years of age, and seven years citizenship. Both senators and representatives must, at the time of their election, be inhabitants of the state for which they are chosen. The time of their previous residence is fixed by the constitutions or laws of the states themselves.

The vice-president of the United States presides over the senate, but has no vote in it, unless they be equally divided. The house of representatives elects its own speaker. The congress meet every second year, on the first Monday of December; in the interval, they may adjourn to such time as they please, so that they meet at least once in each year. But neither house can adjourn for more than three days without the consent of the other; if they disagree, the president fixes the time of adjournment. This, however, has never yet happened. The congress expires on the third of March in every second year. The president may call a special meeting of congress when he thinks it necessary.

Each house of congress is the judge of the elections, returns and qualifications of its own members; it may compel their attendance, punish them for disorderly behaviour, and with the concurrence of two-thirds, expel a member.

No person holding an office under the United States can be a member of either house during his continuance in office; nor can a senator, or representative, during the time for which he was elected, be appointed to any civil office under the United States, created, or the emoluments of which have been increased, during that time. State officers may be elected to congress, when not disabled by the constitution or laws of their own states. In general, state and federal offices are held to be incompatible.

The members of both houses are privileged from arrest, (except for treason, felony, or breach of the peace,) during their attendance at the sessions of their respective houses, and in going and returning from the same. They are not to be questioned, out of congress, for their speeches and debates therein.

Sect. 2.—*Of the Executive Department.*

The executive power is vested in a single magistrate, called the President of the United States. The constitution does not assign to him any council; but he frequently consults the heads of departments, who are officers recognised by the constitution, whom he appoints with the consent of the senate, and whom he may remove at pleasure. The legislature fixes their number and their functions. They are at present four: the secretary of state, whose official duties embrace the foreign and the home department, and those of the treasury, of war, and of the navy. These, with the attorney-general, and of late the postmaster-general, form what is called a cabinet council; which the constitution, however, does not recognise, though it does not forbid. The president is responsible for his acts, and may be impeached for treason, bribery, or other high crimes and misdemeanors.

The president has a qualified negative on the acts of the legislature, and therefore may be considered as a branch of it, though the constitution does not say so in terms; but on the contrary, declares in the first section of its first article, that "*all* legislative powers therein granted shall be vested in a congress of the United States, which shall consist of a senate and house of representatives." But by the seventh section of the same article the president's approbation and signature are required to give effect to any bill, resolution or vote passed by the two houses; and if he objects, the bill, resolution or vote does not take effect, or become a law, unless reconsidered and passed by two-thirds of the senate and of the house of representatives.

There is also a vice-president, who is president of the senate by virtue of his office, and is to exercise the duties of president in case of a vacancy of that office by the death, removal, resignation, or inability of the chief magistrate.

The president and vice-president hold their offices during a term of four years; but may be re-elected as often as the people choose. There is, however, no example of a president or vice-president having served more than two terms; the first president, Washington, having declined a third election, his example has been followed by his successors; and it is now become a popular maxim that a president or vice-president can only be elected for two successive terms.

The election of president and vice-president is made

by ballot, by electors in each state, at the same time, but by different tickets, designating the votes for the respective offices.

The electors are appointed or chosen in each state in such manner as the state legislature directs. In some states the legislatures appoint them themselves by joint or concurrent votes of the two houses; in others, they are elected by the people. Their number is to be equal to the aggregate number of the senators and representatives of each state in the congress of the United States. No member of congress, whether senator or representative, nor any person holding an office of trust or profit under the United States, can be an elector.

The electors, thus chosen, meet in their respective states, and vote by ballot for a president and vice-president, as above mentioned, one of whom, at least, is not to be an inhabitant of the state in which he is chosen. They then transmit their votes, sealed, to the president of the senate, who, on a day appointed by law, (the second Wednesday in February succeeding the meeting of the electors,) opens all the certificates in the presence of both houses of congress, and declares the persons who have the majority of votes, and who are of course elected. If, however, no one should have a majority of votes, the house of representatives shall immediately, if for a president, and the senate if for a vice-president, proceed to choose the former out of the three, and the latter out of the two highest in votes; in which choice the representatives shall vote by states, and the senators individually. If the house do not choose a president before the fourth of March next following, the vice-president shall act as president, as in other cases of vacancy of the president's office.

The congress determines the time of choosing the electors, and the day on which they are to give their votes, which is to be the same throughout the United States. By the existing law, the electors are to meet and vote on the first Wednesday in December, in every fourth year succeeding the last election, and are to be chosen or appointed within thirty-four days preceding the day of their meeting.

On failure of the president by death or otherwise, his duties devolve on the vice-president; and congress may declare by law who shall perform those duties, in case of the failure of both, during the vacancy. The congress have declared by a law that it should be the president pro tempore of the senate; and if there should be none, then the speaker of the house of representatives.

No person, except a natural born citizen, or one who was a citizen of the United States at the time of the adoption of the Constitution, can be elected to the office of president, nor can one be so elected who shall

c

not have attained the age of thirty-five years, and been fourteen years a resident within the United States; and no person constitutionally ineligible to the office of president, can be elected to that of vice-president.

The president is a responsible officer. He is sworn faithfully to execute his office, and to the best of his ability to preserve, protect and defend the constitution. He, as well as the vice-president and all civil officers of the United States, shall be removed on impeachment for and conviction of, treason, bribery, or other high misdemeanors.

Sect. 3.—*Of the Judiciary Department.*

The judiciary power of the United States is vested in a supreme court and such inferior courts as congress from time to time may establish. The judges are appointed by the president, with the advice and consent of the senate. They hold their offices during good behaviour.

The supreme court at present consists of one chief justice and six associate judges, and holds its sittings once a year at the seat of government. There is in each state one, and in some two, district courts, consisting of a single judge, who holds regular sittings four times in the year, and special sessions, whenever occasion requires. Above those tribunals and inferior to the supreme court, there is a circuit court composed of one of the judges of the supreme court, who repairs twice a year to the districts allotted to him, and there sits with the district judge, who, with him, constitutes the circuit court. The states or districts are for that purpose divided into circuits, one of which is allotted to each judge of the supreme court, including the chief justice. A few of the states are without a circuit court, and the district judge performs its functions. Measures are in contemplation to remedy this defect.

During the presidency of the first Adams, a law was passed, in virtue of which three judges were appointed in and for each circuit, who, together, without the district judge, composed the circuit court. On a change of administration, that excellent system was abolished.

Courts martial and the senate, sitting as a court for the trial of impeachments, are not considered as within the ordinary judicial order. They are exceptions to the general system.

SECTION 4.—*Appointment of Officers and Salaries.*

The president nominates, and, with the advice and consent of the senate, appoints ambassadors, other public ministers and consuls, judges of the supreme court and all other officers of the United States, whose appointment are not otherwise provided for by the constitution, and all which shall be established by law; but the congress may also by law vest the appointment of such inferior officers as they think proper, in the president alone, in the courts of law or in the heads of departments.

The president may also fill up all vacancies happening during the recess of the senate, by granting commissions, which shall expire at the end of their next session. If they should so expire in consequence of the president's neglecting to send nominations to the senate in a reasonable time, or of their disagreement, the constitution does not seem to have provided for filling the vacancies.

The president, vice-president, senators, representatives and judges have their salaries fixed by law. Those of the judges cannot be diminished during their continuance in office. That of the president can neither be increased nor diminished; and he shall not receive any other emolument from the United States or any of them. The nation, however, has provided a house for his residence, and furnishes it from time to time. The house and furniture are national property.

Such is the organization of the general government of the United States. We shall now enumerate the powers that are vested in them, and show in what manner those powers are distributed, first laying down,

as a general rule, that all the legislative powers granted by the constitution are vested in the congress, subject to the qualified negative of the president, as abovementioned, which must always be understood when
we speak of the powers vested in congress. That
negative power, or *veto*, as it is called, is not intended
to be frequently used. It is but seldom that a president can have just cause to differ in opinion from the
representatives of the people and those of the states.

CHAPTER IV.

OF THE POWERS, RIGHTS AND DUTIES OF THE GENERAL AND STATE GOVERNMENTS.

SECTION 1.—*Foreign Relations, War, Peace, Treaties.*

CONGRESS have the power of declaring war, and of doing all that may be necessary to carry that declaration into effect, which the constitution thus enumerates: to grant letters of marque and reprisal; to raise and support armies and provide and maintain a navy; to make rules for the government and regulation of the land and naval forces, and concerning captures by land and water; to provide for calling forth the militia, when necessary to execute the laws of the Union, suppress insurrections and repel invasions, and for organizing, arming and disciplining the same, and governing such parts thereof as may be employed in the service of the United States, reserving to the states the appointment of the officers and the authority of training the militia, according to the discipline prescribed by congress; to erect forts, magazines, arsenals, dock-yards and other needful buildings, on sites to be by them purchased, with the consent of the legislatures of the states in which they may be situated.

But, although congress have the power of declaring, and, as we have seen, of *making* war, that of .making peace is not confided to them. The president is the organ of the nation with foreign governments; to him belongs the power of negotiating all treaties, whether of peace, alliance, commerce, neutrality, or of whatever other description. Therefore, the putting an end to a war depends, in the first instance, on his discretion; but no treaty can be valid, unless it receives the concurrent approbation of the senate, by a majority of two-thirds of the members present; and if an appropriation of money, or some act of legislation is necessary to give it effect, then congress must pass a law for such purposes; in every other respect, treaties signed by the president and ratified by the senate, are, after being made known by a proclamation of the president, to be executed as the *supreme law* of the land. A cession of territory, however, would seem to require the consent of the state in which it is situated.

The president of the United States, as the chief executive magistrate of the Union, is, by virtue of his office, commander-in-chief of the army and navy, and also of the militia, when called into the national service: he, with the advice and consent of the senate, sends, and, without such consent, receives ambassadors, ministers of inferior grade, consuls and consular agents, and generally represents, in the view of foreign powers, the *majesty of the nation.* With him alone, or with his

secretary of state, foreign sovereigns and their ministers are allowed to communicate in their public capacities, nor can they appeal from his decisions to any other
authority in the land; but they may apply to the judiciary in matters in which that branch of government
is competent to decide, complying with the forms
which the law requires.

Section 2.—*Finance.*

The congress are authorized to borrow money on
the credit of the United States; to lay and collect
taxes, duties, imposts and excises, without any limitation but that they are to be equal throughout the
United States, and that no duties are to be laid upon
articles exported from any state. All direct taxes are to
be in proportion to the population, as in the election of
representatives. The objects, for which those powers of
taxation are given, are declared to be "to pay the debts
and provide for the *common defence* and *general welfare*
of the United States, which includes every subject of
general interest. It is *now* a settled doctrine that the
money thus raised may be applied by congress to the
making of roads, canals and other public improvements,
provided they be of a *national*, not of a *local* character,
and this doctrine has been acted upon in numerous
instances. The protection of agriculture, commerce
and manufactures against the legislative enactments or
fiscal regulations of foreign nations, seems to be a legiti-

mate object for the exercise of the powers of taxation vested in congress. What would become of our nation, if the government established for the *common defence*, could not *protect* the interests of the citizens against foreign powers, by its legislation as well as by force of arms?

The supreme power over the treasury belongs to the legislature, and therefore no money can be drawn from it but in consequence of appropriations made by law. The congress have moreover the power to coin money and regulate the value thereof, and of foreign coin. All bills for raising revenue must originate in the house of representatives; but the senate may propose or concur with amendments, as in other bills.

Section 3.—*Commerce.*

Congress have the power to regulate commerce with foreign nations, among the several states, and with the Indian tribes, and to fix the standard of weights and measures. This last power, however, they have not yet exercised. They are also empowered to make uniform laws on the subject of bankruptcy throughout the United States.

In execution of the power to regulate trade, and also of that to regulate the value of money, the congress have established a national bank, which has fully answered the object in view. The right of the national legislature to create such an institution has often been, and is still questioned by men whose opinions are entitled to respect; but experience has shown that the value of money cannot be effectually regulated by any other means, through so extensive a country as ours, while each state retains the power of granting to individuals and monied associations the privilege of *issuing bills of credit*, the value of which fluctuates and will fluctuate still more, unless there is some superior power in or under the authority of the national government to check their improvident issues.

On the 4th of April, 1800, an act was passed by congress for establishing a uniform system of bankruptcy throughout the United States. That act was limited to five years, but was not permitted to run through its course; it was repealed on the 19th of December, 1803, wanting little more than one year to expire by its own limitation. Since that time various efforts have been made to revive it, or to obtain an act on similar principles, but all without success; the measure has hitherto appeared to be unpopular with the majority of the people of the United States. The laws of the same description made by the legislatures of the individual states, have been adjudged by the supreme court of the United States to be unconstitutional, (except under restrictions and limitations that would make them beneficially impracticable,) principally on the ground that they *impair*

the obligation of contracts, which, as will be seen hereafter, is prohibited to the states.

The want of laws adequate to the relief of bank-
rupts and their creditors is severely felt throughout the
United States, and there is but little hope of a uniform
system being adopted. As congress are not required
by the constitution to make a *complete* system, but
merely *uniform laws* on the *subject* of bankruptcy, it
might be sufficient, perhaps, if they were to enact some
general rules and principles, leaving the details to the
wisdom of the state legislatures, to be suited by them
to their peculiar circumstances.

SECTION 4.—*General and Penal Legislation.*

The congress, besides the special powers to them
granted, are authorized to make all laws that may
be necessary and proper for carrying into execution
the powers vested in them or in the government of the
United States or in any department or office thereof.

This includes penal legislation for the purpose of
enforcing obedience to their statutes. Independent of
this general power, the constitution gives them a special
authority in particular cases, as 1. To provide for the
punishment of counterfeiting the securities and current
coin of the United States; 2. To define and punish
piracies and felonies committed on the high seas, and

offences against the law of nations. The crime of treason is defined by the constitution itself, and is to consist only "in levying war against the United States, or adhering to their enemies, giving them aid and comfort."

Congress have the power to declare the punishment of treason; but no attainder shall work corruption of blood or forfeiture, except during the life of the person attainted on attainder of treason. *Attainder* here must mean *conviction;* as by a preceding section congress are prohibited from passing bills of attainder. No one can be convicted of treason, but on the testimony of two witnesses to the same overt act, or on confession in open court. The trial of all crimes, (except in cases of impeachment and military offences triable by courts martial) is to be by jury, in the state where the crime has been committed; when out of a state, congress may fix the place of trial.

The pardoning power is vested in the president, except in cases of impeachment; these are tried by the senate. The house of representatives impeaches, and the senate tries. No conviction can take place, unless two-thirds of the members concur. The judgment does not extend further than removal and disqualification from office; but the party may be further prosecuted at law for the same offence.

The constitution, and the laws made in pursuance

thereof, and all treaties made under the authority of the United States are the *supreme law of the land*, anything in the constitution or laws of any state to the contrary notwithstanding.

The president takes care that the laws be faithfully executed.

Section 5.—*Judicial Power.*

The judicial power of the general government, extends to all cases in law and equity arising under the constitution and laws of the United States, and under treaties made by their authority; to cases affecting ambassadors, other public ministers and consuls—to all cases of admiralty and maritime jurisdiction—to controversies, to which the United States shall be a party—to controversies between two or more states —between a state and citizens of another state—between citizens of different states—between citizens of the same state, claiming lands under grants of different states, and between a state, or the citizens thereof, and foreign states, citizens or subjects.

This article, however, has been modified by an amendment to the constitution, which declares that the judicial power of the United States shall not be construed to extend to any suit in law or equity, commenced or prosecuted against one of the United States

D

by citizens of another state, or by foreigners. It has been held that this restriction does not extend to cases of admiralty and maritime jurisdiction.

Except in cases affecting ambassadors, other public ministers and consuls, and those to which a state shall be a party, the supreme court has only appellate jurisdiction, with such exceptions and under such regulations as congress may make. The original jurisdiction is vested by law partly in the circuit and partly in the district courts; the former having an appellate jurisdiction over the district courts in matters within the cognizance of the latter. The manner in which the powers are distributed between these tribunals is too complicated to be explained here. Some of these powers are exercised concurrently with, and others exclusively from the courts of the individual states.

In various instances congress have availed themselves of the aid of the state courts and magistrates to carry their laws or some parts of them into execution. This *auxiliary system* is calculated not only to promote harmony between the general and the state governments, but also to prevent the consolidation of the Union; for were the state authorities to refuse their assistance, congress would be compelled to fill the land with their inferior officers and magistrates, which could not be long tolerated by the people; and a dissolution of the Union might be the fatal consequence.

Section 6.—*New States.*

New states may be admitted by congress into the
Union; but no new state shall be formed or erected
within the jurisdiction of any other state, nor by the
junction of two or more states or parts of states, without the consent of the legislatures of those states as well
as of congress.

Under this power, congress has purchased Louisiana
from France, and Florida from Spain, and erected new
states out of the former territory. Under the same
power the state of Maine has been erected, with the
consent of the legislature of Massachusetts, to which it
formerly belonged. Vermont and Kentucky have in
like manner been erected into states with the consent
of those that had or claimed jurisdiction over them.

Section 7.—*Local Jurisdiction of Congress.*

The congress is empowered to exercise exclusive
legislation in all cases whatsoever, over the district,
not more than ten miles square, where the seat of
government may be established, in virtue of a cession
of territory by particular states. This jurisdiction is
now exercised over the District of Columbia, which
was formerly part of the states of Virginia and Maryland, but has been ceded by those states to the United

States. The congress exercises the same jurisdiction over all places purchased from the states for the erection of forts, magazines, dock-yards and other public buildings.

The congress also may make all necessary rules and regulations respecting the territory or other property belonging to the United States. What is called the territory of the United States, consists of, 1st. the District of Columbia, abovementioned; 2. The forts, arsenals, dock-yards, &c. also abovementioned; 3. Those lands which have been ceded to the United States by Great Britain, by the treaty of peace; by the states, after the conclusion of the said treaty; and by France and Spain under the treaties of cession of Louisiana and Florida, and which not having yet been erected into states, are governed under the authority of the United States, until they shall be admitted into the Union. There are now three territories, each of which is entitled to a delegate in congress, who may join in debates, but not vote. They are Michigan, Arkansas and Florida. The remainder of the lands of the United States to the west and north-west, and beyond the Rocky Mountains are yet wild and uncultivated. A few military posts and some scattered habitations only exist there.

Section 8.—*Miscellaneous Powers of Congress.*

Independent of the powers mentioned in the foregoing

articles, congress have some special ones, which cannot be classed under a general head; such as that of establishing post-offices and post-roads, granting exclusive privileges to authors and inventors for their writings and discoveries and prohibiting the importation of slaves, which last power they have only exercised since the year 1808, the constitution having prohibited them from doing it before that time. The power to make a uniform bankrupt law might have been classed among these; but we have thought that it came more properly under the head of "Commerce." Congress are also empowered to establish a uniform rule for the naturalization of foreigners. This power has been considered as vested in the general government exclusively of the states, which the required *uniformity* appears necessarily to imply. By the existing law, five years residence in the United States are required, before an alien can be naturalized, and he must have declared, two years before, his intention to become a citizen. He must also be proved to be a person of good moral character, and take an oath to support the constitution of the United States, coupled with an express renunciation of his former allegiance. Naturalization may be obtained in the state courts, as well as in those of federal jurisdiction; but it can only be done in execution of a law of congress. There are states where aliens cannot hold real property, which often makes it necessary for them to be naturalized, as by that means they become entitled to all the privileges and rights of natural born

D 2

citizens, except that they cannot be elected to the offices of president and vice-president. This relic of the feudal system, however, has been abolished in some states, and mitigated in others, and will probably soon entirely disappear from our codes.

SECTION 9.—*Protection of the States and Guarantee of Republican Government.*

The United States guarantee to every state in the Union, *a republican form of government.* By this expression we would understand a government "securing civil liberty and equal rights, and founded on the *representative,* to the exclusion of the *hereditary* principle." This, at least, is what we conceive to have been the meaning of the framers of our constitution, with respect to this country, to which alone the words are to be applied. We do not think that the states have a right to require more from each other. The principle of representation necessarily involves those of the sovereignty of the people, and the responsibility of public officers. Every thing else is matter of detail, which may well be left to the wisdom of the states.

The United States are further bound to protect each of the states against invasion, and if required by the legislature of any of them, or by the executive (when the legislature cannot be convened,) against domestic violence.

SECTION 10.—*Restrictions on State and Federal Power.*

No state can enter into any treaty, alliance or confederation; this prohibition is general and unconditional,
and a subsequent clause prohibits the states from making, without the consent of congress, any agreement or
compact with each other; nor can they, without such
consent, engage in war or keep troops or ships of war
in time of peace, unless in case of invasion or imminent
danger, which admits of no delay. They cannot grant
letters of marque and reprisal, coin money, emit bills
of credit, make any thing but gold and silver a tender
in payment of debts, nor pass any law, impairing the
obligation of contracts. These last mentioned prohibitions are absolute and unconditional.

The states cannot, without the consent of congress,
lay any duty on tonnage, nor on imports or exports,
unless that may be absolutely necessary for executing
their inspection laws, which are laws for ascertaining
the merchantable quality of produce, previous to exportation, and which the states are authorized to make.
The net proceeds of all imposts and duties laid by any
state on imports or exports are to be for the use of the
treasury of the United States; and all such laws are to
be subject to the revision and control of congress.

No such imposts or duties have been yet laid by any

of the states; it has not been found necessary for the execution of their inspection laws.

Neither the United States nor the states individually can pass bills of attainder, or ex post facto laws, nor can they grant titles of nobility. No person holding any office of profit or trust under the United States, can, without the consent of congress, accept any present, emolument, office or title of any kind whatever from any king, prince or foreign state.

Congress can make no law respecting an establishment of religion or prohibiting the free exercise thereof, or abridging the freedom of speech or of the press; or the right of the people peaceably to assemble and to petition the government for a redress of grievances.

Besides the above restrictions, there are numerous articles, as well in the constitution as in the amendments to it, in the nature of a bill of rights, and the object of which is to secure the liberty of the citizen, particularly as respects the benefit of the writ of habeas corpus, of trial by jury in civil and criminal cases; the inviolability of domicile, and security from illegal searches and from the obligation of quartering soldiers in time of peace, and other like provisions, by which civil liberty is fully guaranteed.

The enumeration in the constitution of certain rights, is not to be constructed to deny or disparage others retained by the people; and the powers not delegated to the United States by the constitution, nor prohibited by it to the states, are reserved to the states respectively or to the people. This article differs from a similar one in the confederation in this, that the word *expressly* is here left out, which leaves room for implied powers, without the admission of which the constitution could not be carried into effect.

SECTION 11.—*Public Law between the States.*

This is what Tacitus calls *humanitatis commercia*, and what has been still more elegantly called *fœdera generis humani.* Our constitution says but little on this important subject. What it says, however, is susceptible of much developement, and, it is hoped, will receive it. These are the principal features of what it declares:

The citizens of each state are entitled to all the privileges and immunities of citizens in the several states. Fugitives from justice and from personal service or labour, are to be delivered up on being demanded in the manner prescribed by the constitution and the laws made in pursuance thereof.

Full faith and credit are to be given in each state to the public acts, records and judicial proceedings of every other state; and congress may prescribe by law the manner in which such records and proceedings shall be proved, and the effect thereof. Congress have passed a few laws to carry this last clause into execution; but have not yet, by any means, done all that could be done to attain the object that it has in view—the convenience of the citizens.

SECTION 12.—*Mode of amending the Constitution.*

It is the duty of congress to propose amendments to the constitution, whenever two-thirds of both houses deem it necessary; and on the application of the legislatures of the several states, they are bound to call a convention for proposing amendments. In either case, when the amendments proposed are ratified by the legislatures of three-fourths of the several states, or by conventions in three-fourths thereof, as the one or the other mode may be proposed by congress, they become parts of the constitution. No state, however, without its consent, can be deprived of its equal suffrage in the senate.

Fourteen amendments have already been made to the constitution on the proposition of congress in pursuance of these powers, which in the above sketch have been considered as a part of the original instrument, and, therefore, are not otherwise separately noticed. They now form a part of the constitution quite as much as if they had been originally inserted in it.

CHAPTER V.

THUS we have presented to our readers a brief view of the constitution of the United States, which, on cool and mature reflection, we cannot help considering as the most perfect system of government that has ever existed among mankind. It has, as far as it has gone, solved the problem of the possibility of the existence of a republic in a widely extended country, and the means, never thought of before, has been found to effect that which was considered as next to impossible, the combination of the federal and national systems of government, so nicely and so skilfully balanced, that one does not seem to preponderate over the other. It was a bold thought of the framers of this instrument to vest the dreaded powers of the *purse* and the *sword* in the hands of the national congress, which far from producing the mischiefs that were anticipated by some, has given strength and power to the United States, and left the states of which the Union is composed, possessed of as much freedom, sovereignty and independence as is necessary for their happiness and welfare, and the preservation of their liberties.

If we consider the constitution in respect to its organization, we shall find the most perfect balance between the two apparently opposite principles of national and state sovereignty. The senate, from its equality of votes and the mode of election of its members, is the natural guardian of the sovereignty of the states, while the popular branch of the national legislature, naturally hostile to the encroachments of power, will watch over the rights and liberties of the people. Both are the offspring of the states, to which at short intervals they must return.

Nor is the distribution of powers between the federal and the state governments less worthy of admiration. At first view, it might appear, as if these powers were most unequally distributed. The supreme rights of empire, *jura summi imperii*, as they are called, with the purse and the sword, as the means for carrying them into execution, have a formidable aspect; and it would seem as if the national government could easily swallow up the sovereignty of the states. But the danger, if any there be, seems rather to be on the other side. The independent organization of the state governments with their legislatures, governors, militia, judiciary and ministerial officers, with uncontrolled jurisdiction within their constitutional limits; the very name of that sovereignty and independence, which they possess in a great degree, and of which they are excessively jealous; the means they have in their power of collecting and combining their force without the appearance of illegality; all these things form a strong counterpoise to the authority of the general government, which with all its ample powers, operates but little on the individual citizens, whereas the state officers are constantly in contact with them, and have greater means of securing their attachment. The national government, as we have before observed, is frequently obliged to require the aid of the state authorities to carry its laws into effect; and on the continuance of this *auxiliary system*, as we have already observed, depends in a great measure the preservation of the Union, as it now exists.

This Union has already experienced severe trials, but has come off victorious from them all. Nor is there any real danger to be apprehended, while the people remain virtuous, and true to themselves. What ambition and luxury and the increasing spirit of party may produce in a series of years, it is impossible to foretell. All that the patriot can do, is to wish that the period of the dissolution of this happy Union may be protracted to the end of time.

E

APPENDIX.

No. I.

DECLARATION OF INDEPENDENCE.

In Congress, July 4, 1776.

The unanimous Declaration of the thirteen United States of America.

WHEN, in the course of human events, it becomes necessary for one people to dissolve the political bands which have connected them with another, and to assume, among the powers of the earth, the separate and equal station to which the laws of nature and nature's God entitle them, a decent respect to the opinions of mankind requires, that they should declare the causes which impel them to the separation.

We hold these truths to be self-evident:—that all men are created equal; that they are endowed by their Creator with certain unalienable rights; that among these are life, liberty, and the pursuit of happiness. That to secure these rights, governments are instituted among men, deriving their just powers from the consent of the governed; that whenever any form of government becomes destructive of these ends, it is the right of the people to alter or to abolish it, and to institute a new government, laying its foundation on such principles, and organizing its powers in such form as to them shall seem most likely to effect their safety and happiness. Prudence, indeed, will dictate, that governments long established should not be changed for light and transient causes; and accordingly all experience hath shown, that mankind are more disposed to suffer while evils are sufferable, than to right themselves by abolishing the forms to which they are accustomed. But when a long train of abuses and usurpations, pursuing invariably the same object, evinces a design to reduce them under absolute despotism, it is their right, it is their duty, to throw off such government, and to provide new guards for their future security. Such has been the patient sufferance of these colonies; and such is now the necessity which constrains them to alter their former systems of government. The history of the present king of Great Britain is a history of repeated injuries and usurpations, all having in direct object the establishment of an absolute tyranny over these states. To prove this, let facts be submitted to a candid world.

He has refused his assent to laws the most wholesome and necessary for the public good.

He has forbidden his governors to pass laws of immediate and pressing importance, unless suspended in their operation, till his assent should be obtained; and when so suspended, he has utterly neglected to attend to them. He has refused to pass other laws for the accommodation of large districts of people, unless those people would relinquish the right of representation in the legislature—a right inestimable to them, and formidable to tyrants only.

He has called together legislative bodies at places unusual, uncomfortable, and distant from the repository of their public records, for the sole purpose of fatiguing them into compliance with his measures.

He has dissolved representative houses repeatedly, for opposing, with manly firmness, his invasions on the rights of the people.

He has refused, for a long time after such dissolutions, to cause others to be elected; whereby the legislative powers, incapable of annihilation, have returned to the people at large for their exercise, the state remaining, in the mean time, exposed to all the dangers of invasion from without and convulsions within.

He has endeavoured to prevent the population of these states; for that purpose obstructing the laws of naturalization of foreigners; refusing to pass others to encourage their migration hither, and raising the conditions of new appropriations of lands.

He has obstructed the administration of justice, by refusing his assent to laws for establishing judiciary powers.

He has made judges dependent on his will alone, for the tenure of their offices, and the amount and payment of their salaries.

He has erected a multitude of new offices, and sent hither swarms of officers, to harass our people, and eat out their substance.

He has kept among us, in times of peace, standing armies, without the consent of our legislatures.

He has affected to render the military independent of, and superior to, the civil power.

He has combined with others to subject us to a jurisdiction foreign to our Constitution, and unacknowledged by our laws; giving his assent to their acts of pretended legislation:

For quartering large bodies of armed troops among us:

For protecting them, by a mock trial, from punishment for any murders which they should commit on the inhabitants of these States:

For cutting off our trade with all parts of the world:

For imposing taxes on us without our consent:

For depriving us, in many cases, of the benefits of trial by jury:

For transporting us beyond seas to be tried for pretended offences:

For abolishing the free system of English laws in a neigh-

E 2

bouring province, establishing therein an arbitrary government, and enlarging its boundaries, so as to render it at once an example and fit instrument for introducing the same absolute rule into these colonies.

For taking away our charters, abolishing our most valuable laws, and altering, fundamentally, the forms of our governments:

For suspending our own legislatures, and declaring themselves invested with power to legislate for us in all cases whatsoever.

He has abdicted government here, by declaring us out of his protection, and waging war against us.

He has plundered our seas, ravaged our coasts, burnt our towns, and destroyed the lives of our people.

He is at this time transporting large armies of foreign mercenaries to complete the works of death, desolation, and tyranny, already begun with circumstances of cruelty and perfidy, scarcely paralleled in the most barbarous ages, and totally unworthy the head of a civilized nation.

He has constrained our fellow citizens, taken captive on the high seas, to bear arms against their country, to become the executioners of their friends and brethren, or to fall themselves by their hands.

He has excited domestic insurrections amongst us, and has endeavoured to bring on the inhabitants of our frontiers the merciless Indian savages, whose known rule of warfare is an undistinguished destruction of all ages, sexes, and conditions.

In every stage of these oppressions we have petitioned for redress in the most humble terms: our repeated petitions have been answered only by repeated injury. A prince, whose character is thus marked by every act which may define a tyrant, is unfit to be the ruler of a free people.

Nor have we been wanting in attentions to our British brethren. We have warned them, from time to time, of attempts by their legislature to extend an unwarrantable jurisdiction over us. We have reminded them of the circumstances of our emigration and settlement here. We have appealed to their native justice and magnanimity, and we have conjured them by the ties of our common kindred to disavow these usurpations, which would inevitably interrupt our connexions and correspondence. They too have been deaf to the voice of justice and of consanguinity. We must, therefore, acquiesce in the necessity which denounces our separation, and hold them, as we hold the rest of mankind—enemies in war, in peace friends.

We, therefore, the representatives of the United States of America, in general congress assembled, appealing to the Supreme Judge of the world, for the rectitude of our intentions, do, in the name and by the authority of the good people of these colonies, solemnly publish and declare, that these united colonies are, and of right ought to be, free and independent States; that they are absolved from all allegiance to the British crown, and that all political connexion between them and the State of Great Britain is, and ought to be, totally dissolved; and that, as free and independent States, they have full power to levy war, conclude peace, contract alliances, establish commerce, and to do all other acts and things which independent States may of right do. And for the support of this declaration, with a firm reliance on the protection of Divine Providence, we mutually pledge to each other our lives, our fortunes, and our sacred honour.

JOHN HANCOCK.

NEW HAMPSHIRE.
Josiah Bartlett,
William Whipple,
Matthew Thornton.

MASSACHUSETTS BAY.
Samuel Adams,
John Adams,
Robert Treat Paine,
Elbridge Gerry.

RHODE ISLAND, etc.
Stephen Hopkins,
William Ellery.

CONNECTICUT.
Roger Sherman,
Samuel Huntingdon,
William Williams,
Oliver Wolcott.

NEW YORK.
William Floyd,
Philip Livingston,
Francis Lewis,
Lewis Morris.

NEW JERSEY.
Richard Stockton,
John Witherspoon,
Francis Hopkinson,
John Hart,
Abraham Clark.

PENNSYLVANIA.
Robert Morris,
Benjamin Rush,
Benjamin Franklin,
John Morton,
George Clymer,
James Smith,
George Taylor,
James Wilson,
George Ross.

DELAWARE.
Cæsar Rodney,
George Read,
Thomas M'Kean.

MARYLAND.
Samuel Chase,
William Paca,
Thomas Stone,
C. Carroll, of Carrolton.

VIRGINIA.
George Wythe,
Richard Henry Lee,
Thomas Jefferson,
Benjamin Harrison,
Thomas Nelson, jr.
Francis Lightfoot Lee,
Carter Braxton.

NORTH CAROLINA.
William Hooper,
Joseph Hewes,
John Penn.

SOUTH CAROLINA.
Edward Rutledge,
Thomas Heyward, jr.
Thomas Lynch, jr.
Arthur Middleton.

GEORGIA.
Burton Gwinnet,
Lyman Hall,
George Walton.

No. II.

___

ARTICLES OF CONFEDERATION.

___

In Congress, July 8, 1778.

ARTICLES OF CONFEDERATION AND PERPETUAL UNION

Between the States of New Hampshire, Massachusetts Bay, Rhode Island and Providence Plantations, Connecticut, New York, New Jersey, Pennsylvania, Delaware, Maryland, Virginia, North Carolina, South Carolina, and Georgia.

ARTICLE 1. The style of this confederacy shall be, "*The United States of America.*"

ART. 2. Each State retains its sovereignty, freedom and independence, and every power, jurisdiction, and right, which is not by this confederation, expressly delegated to the United States, in congress assembled.

ART. 3. The said States hereby severally enter into a firm league of friendship with each other, for their common defence, the security of their liberties, and their mutual and general welfare, binding themselves to assist each other against all force offered to, or attacks made upon them, or any of them, on account of religion, sovereignty, trade, or any other pretence whatever.

ART. 4. § 1. The better to secure and perpetuate mutual friendship and intercourse among the people of the different States in this Union, the free inhabitants of each of these States, paupers, vagabonds and fugitives from justice excepted, shall be entitled to all privileges and immunities of free citizens in the several States; and the people of each State shall have free ingress and regress to and from any other State, and shall enjoy therein all the privileges of trade and commerce, subject to the same duties, impositions and restrictions, as the inhabitants thereof respectively; provided that such restrictions shall not extend so far as to prevent the removal of property imported into any State, to any other State, of which the owner is an inhabitant; provided also, that no imposition, duties, or restriction, shall be laid by any State on the property of the United States, or either of them.

§ 2. If any person guilty of, or charged with treason, felony, or other high misdemeanor in any State, shall flee from justice, and be found in any of the United States, he shall, upon the demand of the governor or executive power of the State from which he fled, be delivered up, and removed to the State having jurisdiction of his offence.

§ 3. Full faith and credit shall be given, in each of these States, to the records, acts, and judicial proceedings of the courts and magistrates of every other State.

ART. 5. § 1. For the more convenient management of the general interests of the United States, delegates shall be annually appointed in such a manner as the legislature of each State shall direct, to meet in Congress on the first Monday in November, in every year, with a power reserved to each State to recall its delegates, or any of them, at any time within the year, and to send others in their stead, for the remainder of the year.

§ 2. No State shall be represented in Congress by less than two, nor more than seven members; and no person shall be capable of being a delegate for more than three years, in any term of six years; nor shall any person, being a delegate, be capable of holding any office under the United States, for which he, or any other for his benefit, receives any salary, fees or emolument of any kind.

§ 3. Each State shall maintain its own delegates in a meeting of the States, and while they act as members of the committee of these States.

§ 4. In determining questions in the United States in congress assembled, each State shall have one vote.

§ 5. Freedom of speech and debate in congress shall not be impeached or questioned in any court or place out of congress, and the members of congress shall be protected in their persons from arrests and imprisonments during the time of their going to and from, and attendance on congress, except for treason, felony or breach of the peace.

ART. 6. § 1. No State, without the consent of the United States, in congress assembled, shall send any embassy to, or receive any embassy from, or enter into any conference, agreement, alliance or treaty, with any king, prince or State, nor shall any person holding any office of profit or trust under the United States, or any of them, accept of any present, emolument, office or title, of any kind whatever, from any king, prince or foreign State; nor shall the United States, in congress assembled, or any of them, grant any title of nobility.

§ 2. No two or more States shall enter into any treaty, confederation or alliance whatever, between them, without the consent of the United States, in congress assembled, specifying accurately the purposes for which the same is to be entered into, and how long it shall continue.

§ 3. No State shall lay any imposts or duties which may interfere with any stipulations in treaties, entered into by the United States, in congress assembled, with any king, prince or State, in pursuance of any treaties already proposed by congress to the courts of France and Spain.

§ 4. No vessels of war shall be kept up in time of peace by any State, except such number only as shall be deemed necessary by the United States, in congress assembled, for the defence of such State, or its trade: nor shall any body of forces be kept up, by any State, in time of peace, except such number only as, in the judgment of the United States, in congress assembled, shall be deemed requisite to garrison the forts necessary for the defence of such State; but every State shall always keep up a regular and well disciplined militia, sufficiently armed and accoutred, and shall provide and constantly have ready for use, in public stores, a due number of field pieces and tents, and a proper quantity of arms, ammunition and camp equipage.

§ 5. No State shall engage in any war without the consent of the United States, in congress assembled, unless such State be actually invaded by enemies, or shall have received certain advice of a resolution being formed by some nation of Indians to invade such State, and the danger is so imminent as not to admit of delay till the United States, in congress assembled, can be consulted; nor shall any State grant commissions to any ships or vessels of war, nor letters of marque or reprisal, except it be after a declaration of war by the United States, in Congress assembled, and then only against the kingdom or State, and the subjects thereof, against which war has been so declared, and under such regulations as shall be established by the United States, in congress assembled, unless such State be infested by pirates, in which case vessels of war may be fitted out for that occasion, and kept so long as the danger shall continue, or until the United States, in congress assembled, shall determine otherwise.

ART. 7. When land forces are raised by any State, for the common defence, all officers of, or under the rank of colonel, shall be appointed by the legislature of each State respectively by whom such forces shall be raised, or in such manner as such State shall direct, and all vacancies shall be filled up by the State which first made the appointment.

ART. 8. All charges of war, and all other expenses that shall be incurred for the common defence or general welfare, and allowed by the United States, in congress assembled, shall be defrayed out of a common treasury, which shall be supplied by the several States, in proportion to the value of all land within each State, granted to or surveyed for any person, as such land and the buildings and improvements thereon shall be estimated, according to such mode as the United States, in congress assembled, shall, from time to time, direct and appoint. The taxes for paying that proportion shall be laid and levied by the authority and direction of the legislatures of the several States, within the time agreed upon by the United States, in congress assembled.

ART. 9. § 1. The United States, in congress assembled, shall have the sole and exclusive right and power of determining on peace and war, except in the cases mentioned in the sixth Article, of sending and receiving ambassadors; entering into treaties and alliances, provided that no treaty of commerce shall be made, whereby the legislative power of the respective States shall be restrained from imposing such imposts and duties on foreigners, as their own people are subjected to, or from prohibiting the exportation or importation of any species of goods or commodities whatsoever; of establishing rules for deciding in all cases, what captures on land or water shall be legal, and in what manner prizes taken by land or naval forces in the service of the United States, shall be divided or appropriated; of granting letters of marque and reprisal in times of peace; appointing courts for the trial of piracies and felonies committed on the high seas; and establishing courts for receiving and determining finally appeals in all cases of captures; provided that no member of congress shall be appointed a judge of any of the said courts.

§ 2. The United States, in congress assembled, shall also be the last resort on appeal, in all disputes and differences now subsisting, or that hereafter may arise between two or more States concerning boundary, jurisdiction, or any other cause whatever; which authority shall always be exercised in the manner following: Whenever the legislative or executive authority, or lawful agent of any State in controversy with another, shall present a petition to congress, stating the matter in

F

question, and praying for a hearing, notice thereof shall be given by order of congress, to the legislative or executive authority of the other State in controversy, and a day assigned for the appearance of the parties by their lawful agents, who shall then be directed to appoint, by joint consent, commissioners or judges to constitute a court for hearing and determining the matter in question; but if they cannot agree, congress shall name three persons out of each of the United States, and from the list of such persons each party shall alternately strike out one, the petitioners beginning, until the number shall be reduced to thirteen; and from that number not less than seven, nor more than nine names, as congress shall direct, shall, in the presence of congress, be drawn out by lot; and the persons whose names shall be so drawn, or any five of them, shall be commissioners or judges to hear and finally determine the controversy, so always as a major part of the judges, who shall hear the cause, shall agree in the determination: and if either party shall neglect to attend at the day appointed, without showing reasons which congress shall judge sufficient, or being present, shall refuse to strike, the congress shall proceed to nominate three persons out of each State, and the secretary of congress shall strike in behalf of such party absent or refusing; and the judgment and sentence of the court, to be appointed in the manner before prescribed, shall be final and conclusive; and if any of the parties shall refuse to submit to the authority of such court, or to appear or defend their claim or cause, the court shall nevertheless proceed to pronounce sentence, or judgment, which shall in like manner be final and decisive; the judgment or sentence and other proceedings being in either case transmitted to congress, and lodged among the acts of congress, for the security of the parties concerned; provided, that every commissioner, before he sits in judgment, shall take an oath, to be administered by one of the judges of the supreme or superior court of the State where the cause shall be tried, "well and truly to hear and determine the matter in question, according to the best of his judgment, without favour, affection or hope of reward." Provided also, that no State shall be deprived of territory for the benefit of the United States.

§ 3. All controversies concerning the private right of soil claimed under different grants of two or more States, whose jurisdiction, as they may respect such lands, and the States which passed such grants are adjusted, the said grants or either of them being at the same time claimed to have originated antecedent to such settlement of jurisdiction, shall, on the petition of either party to the congress of the United States, be finally determined, as near as may be, in the same manner as is before prescribed for deciding disputes respecting territorial jurisdiction between different States.

§ 4. The United States in congress assembled shall also have the sole and exclusive right and power of regulating the alloy and value of coin struck by their own authority, or by that of the respective States; fixing the standard of weights and measures throughout the United States; regulating the trade and managing all affairs with the Indians, not members of any of the States; provided that the legislative right of any State, within its own limits, be not infringed or violated; establishing and regulating post offices from one State to another, throughout all the United States, and exacting such postage on the papers passing through the same, as may be requisite to defray the expenses of the said office; appointing all officers of the land forces in the service of the United States, excepting regimental officers; appointing all the officers of the naval forces, and commissioning all officers whatever in the service of the United States; making rules for the government and regulation of the said land and naval forces, and directing their operations.

§ 5. The United States, in congress assembled, shall have authority to appoint a committee, to sit in the recess of congress, to be denominated, "A Committee of the States," and to consist of one delegate from each State; and to appoint such other committees and civil officers as may be necessary for managing the general affairs of the United States under their direction; to appoint one of their number to preside; provided that no person be allowed to serve in the office of president more than one year in any term of three years; to ascertain the necessary sums of money to be raised for the service of the United States, and to appropriate and apply the same for defraying the public expenses; to borrow money or emit bills on the credit of the United States, transmitting every half year to the respective States an account of the sums of money so borrowed or emitted; to build and equip a navy; to agree upon the number of land forces, and to make requisitions from each State for its quota, in proportion to the number of white inhabitants in such State, which requisition shall be binding; and thereupon the legislature of each State shall appoint the regimental officers, raise the men, clothe, arm, and equip them, in a soldier-like manner, at the expense of the United States; and the officers and men so clothed, armed, and equipped, shall march to the place appointed, and within the time agreed on by the United States, in congress assembled; but if the United States, in congress assembled shall, on consideration of circumstances, judge proper that any State should not raise men, or should raise a smaller number than its quota, and that any other State should raise a greater number of men than the quota thereof, such extra number shall be raised, officered, clothed, armed, and equipped in the same manner as the quota of such State, unless the legislature of such State shall judge that such extra number cannot be safely spared out of the same, in which case they shall raise, officer, clothe, arm, and equip, as many of such extra number as they judge can be safely spared, and the officers and men so clothed, armed, and equipped, shall march to the place appointed, and within the time agreed on by the United States in congress assembled.

§ 6. The United States in congress assembled shall never engage in a war, nor grant letters of marque and reprisal in time of peace, nor enter in any treaties or alliances, nor coin money, nor regulate the value thereof, nor ascertain the sums and expenses necessary for the defence and welfare of the United States, or any of them, nor emit bills, nor borrow money on the credit of the United States, nor appropriate money, nor agree upon the number of vessels of war to be built or purchased, or the number of land or sea forces to be raised, nor appoint a commander-in-chief of the army or navy, unless nine States assent to the same, nor shall a question on any other point, except for adjourning from day to day, be determined, unless by the votes of a majority of the United States in congress assembled.

§ 7. The congress of the United States shall have power to adjourn to any time within the year, and to any place within the United States, so that no period of adjournment be for a longer duration than the space of six months, and shall publish the journal of their proceedings monthly, except such parts thereof relating to treaties, alliances, or military operations, as in their judgment require secrecy; and the yeas and nays of the delegates of each State, on any question, shall be entered on the journal, when it is desired by any delegate; and the delegates of a State, or any of them, at his or their request, shall be furnished with a transcript of the said journal, except such parts as are above excepted, to lay before the legislatures of the several States.

Art. 10. The committee of the States, or any nine of them, shall be authorized to execute, in the recess of congress, such of the powers of congress as the United States, in congress assembled, by the consent of nine States, shall, from time to time, think expedient to vest them with; provided that no power be delegated to the said committee, for the exercise of which, by the articles of confederation, the voice of nine States, in the congress of the United States assembled, is requisite.

Art. 11. Canada acceding to this confederation, and joining in the measures of the United States, shall be admitted into, and entitled to all the advantages of this Union: but no other colony shall be admitted into the same, unless such admission be agreed to by nine States.

Art. 12. All bills of credit emitted, moneys borrowed, and

F 2

debts contracted by or under the authority of congress, before the assembling of the United States, in pursuance of the present confederation, shall be deemed and considered as a charge against the United States, for payment and satisfaction whereof the said United States and the public faith are hereby solemnly pledged.

ART. 13. Every State shall abide by the determination of the United States, in congress assembled, in all questions which by this confederation are submitted to them. And the articles of this confederation shall be inviolably observed by every State, and the Union shall be perpetual; nor shall any alteration at any time hereafter be made in any of them, unless such alteration be agreed to in a congress of the United States, and be afterwards confirmed by the legislature of every State.

And whereas it hath pleased the great Governor of the world to incline the hearts of the legislatures we respectively represent in congress, to approve of, and to authorize us to ratify the said articles of confederation and perpetual Union, Know ye, that we, the undersigned delegates, by virtue of the power and authority to us given for that purpose, do, by these presents, in the name and behalf of our respective constituents, fully and entirely ratify and confirm each and every of the said articles of confederation and perpetual union, and all and singular the matters and things therein contained. And we do further solemnly plight and engage the faith of our respective constituents, that they shall abide by the determination of the United States, in congress assembled, in all questions which by the said confederation are submitted to them; and that the articles thereof shall be inviolably observed by the States we respectively represent, and that the Union shall be perpetual. In witness whereof, we have hereunto set our hands, in congress.

Done at Philadelphia, in the State of Pennsylvania, the 9th day of July, in the year of our Lord, 1778, and in the third year of the Independence of America.

NEW HAMPSHIRE.
Josiah Bartlett,
John Wentworth, jr.

MASSACHUSETTS BAY.
Iohn Hancock,
Samuel Adams,
Elbridge Gerry,
Francis Dana,
James Lovel,
Samuel Holten.

RHODE ISLAND, etc.
William Ellery,
Henry Marchant,
John Collins.

CONNECTICUT.
Roger Sherman,
Samuel Huntington,
Oliver Wolcott,
Titus Hosmer,
Andrew Adams.

NEW YORK.
Jas. Duane,
Fra. Lewis,
Wm. Duer,
Gouv. Morris.

NEW JERSEY.
Jno. Witherspoon,
Nath. Scudder.

PENNSYLVANIA.
Robert Morris,
Daniel Roberdeau,

Jona. Bayard Smith,
William Clingan,
Joseph Reed.

DELAWARE.
Thomas M'Kean,
John Dickinson,
Nicholas Van Dyke.

MARYLAND.
John Hanson,
Daniel Carroll.

VIRGINIA.
Richard Henry Lee,
John Banister,
Thomas Adams,
Jno. Harvie,
Francis Lightfoot Lee.

NORTH CAROLINA.
John Penn,
Cons. Harnett,
Jno. Williams.

SOUTH CAROLINA.
Henry Laurens,
William Henry Drayton,
Jno. Mathews,
Richard Hutson,
Thomas Heyward, jr.

GEORGIA.
Jno. Walton,
Edwd. Telfair,
Edwd. Langworthy.

No. III.

———

CONSTITUTION

OF THE

UNITED STATES OF AMERICA.

—·—

We, the people *of the United States, in order to form a more perfect Union, establish justice, insure domestic tranquillity, provide for the common defence, promote the general welfare, and secure the blessings of liberty to ourselves, and our posterity, do ordain and establish this* Constitution *for the United States of America.*

Article I.

Sec. 1. All legislative powers herein granted, shall be vested in a congress of the United States, which shall consist of a senate and house of representatives.

Sec. 2. The house of representatives shall be composed of members chosen every second year by the people of the several states; and the electors in each State shall have the qualifications requisite for electors of the most numerous branch of the legislature.

No person shall be a representative who shall not have attained to the age of twenty-five years, and have been seven years a citizen of the United States, and who shall not, when elected, be an inhabitant of that State in which he shall be chosen.

Representatives and direct taxes shall be apportioned among the several States which may be included within this Union, according to their respective numbers, which shall be determined by adding to the whole number of free persons, including those bound to service for a term of years, and excluding Indians not taxed, three-fifths of all other persons. The actual enumeration shall be made within three years after the first meeting of the congress of the United States, and within every subsequent term of ten years, in such manner as they shall by law direct. The number of representatives shall not exceed one for every thirty thousand, but each State shall have at least one representative; and until such enumeration shall be made, the State of New Hampshire shall be entitled to choose three; Massachusetts, eight; Rhode Island and Providence Plantations, one; Connecticut, five; New York, six; New Jersey, four; Pennsylvania, eight; Delaware, one; Maryland, six; Virginia, ten; North Carolina, five; South Carolina, five, and Georgia, three.

When vacancies happen in the representations from any state, the executive authority thereof shall issue writs of election to fill such vacancies.

The house of representatives shall choose their speaker and other officers, and have the sole power of impeachment.

Sec. 3. The senate of the United States shall be composed of two senators from each State, chosen by the legislature thereof, for six years; each senator shall have one vote.

Immediately after they shall be assembled in consequence of the first election, they shall be divided as equally as may be into three classes. The seats of the senators of the first class shall be vacated at the expiration of the second year, of the second class at the expiration of the fourth year, and of the third class at the expiration of the sixth year; so that one-third may be chosen every second year; and if vacancies happen by resignation, or otherwise, during the recess of the legislature of any State, the executive thereof may make temporary appointments until the next meeting of the legislatures which shall then fill such vacancies.

No person shall be a senator who shall not have attained to the age of thirty years, and been nine years a citizen of the United States, and who shall not, when elected, be an inhabitant of that state for which he shall be chosen.

The vice-president of the United States shall be president of the senate, but shall have no vote, unless they be equally divided.

The senate shall choose their other officers, and also a president *pro tempore*, in the absence of the vice-president, or when he shall exercise the office of president of the United States.

The senate shall have the sole power to try all impeachments. When sitting for that purpose, they shall be on oath or affirmation. When the president of the United States is tried, the chief justice shall preside; and no person shall be convicted without the concurrence of two-thirds of the members present.

Judgment in cases of impeachment shall not extend further than to the removal from office, and disqualification to hold and enjoy any office of honour, trust or profit, under the United States; but the party convicted shall nevertheless be liable and subject to indictment, trial, judgment and punishment according to law.

Sec. 4. The time, places and manner of holding elections for senators and representatives, shall be prescribed in each State by the legislature thereof. But the congress may at any time by law make or alter such regulations, except as to the places of choosing senators.

The congress shall assemble at least once in every year, and such meeting shall be on the first Monday in December, unless they shall by law appoint a different day.

Sec. 5. Each house shall be the judge of the elections, returns and qualifications of its own members, and a majority of each shall constitute a quorum to do business; but a smaller number may adjourn from day to day, and may be authorized to compel the attendance of absent members, in such manner, and under such penalties, as each house may provide.

Each house may determine the rules of its proceedings, punish its members for disorderly behaviour, and, with the concurrence of two-thirds, expel a member.

Each house shall keep a journal of its proceedings, and from time to time publish the same, excepting such parts as may, in their judgment, require secrecy; and the yeas and nays of the members of either house on any question, shall, at the desire of one-fifth of those present, be entered on the journal.

Neither house, during the session of congress, shall, without the consent of the other, adjourn for more than three days, nor to any other place than that in which the two houses shall be sitting.

Sec. 6. The senators and representatives shall receive a compensation for their services, to be ascertained by law, and paid out of the treasury of the United States. They shall in all cases, except treason, felony and breach of the peace, be privileged from arrest during their attendance at the session of their respective houses, and in going to and returning from the same; and for any speech or debate in either house, they shall not be questioned in any other place.

No senator or representative shall, during the time for which he was elected, be appointed to any civil office under the authority of the United States, which shall have been created, or the emoluments whereof shall have been increased during such time; and no person holding any office under the United States, shall be a member of either house during his continuance in office.

Sec. 7. All bills for raising revenue shall originate in the house of representatives; but the senate may propose or concur with amendments as on other bills.

Every bill which shall have passed the house of representatives and the senate, shall, before it becomes a law, be presented to the president of the United States: If he approve he shall sign it; but if not he shall return it, with his objections, to that house in which it shall have originated, who shall enter the objections at large on their journal, and proceed to reconsider it. If after such reconsideration, two-thirds of that house shall agree to pass the bill, it shall be sent, together with the objections, to the other house, by which it shall likewise be reconsidered, and if approved by two-thirds of that house, it shall become a law. But in all such cases, the votes of both houses shall be determined by yeas and nays; and the names of the persons voting for and against the bill, shall be entered on the journal of each house respectively. If any bill shall not be returned by the president within ten days (Sundays excepted) after it shall have been presented to him, the same shall be a law, in like manner as if he had signed it, unless the congress, by their adjournment, prevent its return, in which case it shall not be a law.

Every order, resolution or vote, to which the concurrence of the senate and house of representatives may be necessary (except on a question of adjournment) shall be presented to the president of the United States; and before the same shall take effect, shall be approved by him, or being disapproved by him, shall be repassed by two-thirds of the senate and house of representatives, according to the rules and limitations prescribed in the case of a bill.

Sec. 8. The congress shall have power

To lay and collect taxes, duties, imposts and excises; to pay the debts and provide for the common defence and general welfare of the United States; but all duties, imposts and excises shall be uniform throughout the United States:

To borrow money on the credit of the United States:

To regulate commerce with foreign nations, and among the several states, and with the Indian tribes:

To establish a uniform rule of naturalization, and uniform laws on the subject of bankruptcies throughout the United States;

To coin money, regulate the value thereof, and of foreign coin, and to fix the standard of weights and measures:

To provide for the punishment of counterfeiting the securities and current coin of the United States:

To establish post offices and post roads:

To promote the progress of science and useful arts, by securing, for limited times, to authors and inventors, the exclusive right to their respective writings and discoveries:

To constitute tribunals inferior to the supreme court:

To define and punish piracies and felonies committed on the high seas, and offences against the law of nations:

To declare war, grant letters of marque and reprisal, and make rules concerning captures on land and water:

To raise and support armies; but no appropriation of money to that use shall be for a longer term than two years:

To provide and maintain a navy:

To make rules for the government and regulation of the land and naval forces:

To provide for calling forth the militia to execute the laws of he Union, suppress insurrections, and repel invasions:

To provide for organizing, arming and disciplining the militia, and for governing such part of them as may be employed in the service of the United States, reserving to the states respectively, the appointment of the officers, and the authority of training the militia according to the discipline prescribed by congress:

To exercise exclusive legislation in all cases whatsoever, over such district (not exceeding ten miles square) as may, by cession of particular states, and the acceptance of congress, become the seat of government of the United States, and to exercise like authority over all places purchased by the consent of the legislature of the state in which the same shall be, for the erection of forts, magazines, arsenals, dock-yards, and other needful buildings:—And

To make all laws which shall be necessary and proper for carrying into execution the foregoing powers, and all other

G

powers vested by this constitution in the government of the United States, or in any department or officer thereof.

Sec. 9. The migration or importation of such persons as any of the states now existing shall think proper to admit, shall not be prohibited by the congress prior to the year one thousand eight hundred and eight; but a tax or duty may be imposed on such importation, not exceeding ten dollars for each person.

The privileges of the writ of *habeas corpus* shall not be suspended, unless when, in cases of rebellion or invasion, the public safety may require it.

No bill of attainder or *ex post facto* law shall be passed.

No capitation, or other direct tax shall be laid, unless in proportion to the census or enumeration herein before directed to be taken.

No tax or duty shall be laid on articles exported from any State. No preference shall be given by any regulation of commerce or revenue to the ports of one State over those of another: Nor shall vessels bound to, or from one State, be obliged to enter, clear, or pay duties in another.

No money shall be drawn from the treasury, but in consequence of appropriations made by law; and a regular statement and account of the receipts and expenditures of all public money shall be published from time to time.

No title of nobility shall be granted by the United States: and no person holding any office of profit or trust under them, shall, without the consent of the congress, accept of any present, emolument, office, or title of any kind whatever, from any king, prince, or foreign State.

Sec. 10. No state shall enter into any treaty, alliance or confederation; grant letters of marque and reprisal; coin money; emit bills of credit; make any thing but gold and silver coin a tender in the payment of debts, pass any bills of attainder, *ex post facto* law, or law impairing the obligation of contracts, or grant any title of nobility.

No State shall, without the consent of congress, lay any imposts or duties on imports or exports, except what may be absolutely necessary for executing its inspection laws; and the neat produce of all duties and imposts laid by any State on imports or exports, shall be for the use of the treasury of the United States; and all such laws shall be subject to the revision and control of the congress. No State shall, without the consent of congress, lay any duty of tonnage, keep troops, or ships of war, in time of peace, enter into any agreement or compact with another State, or with a foreign power, or engage in war, unless actually invaded, or in such imminent danger as will not admit of delay.

Article II.

Sec. 1. The executive power shall be vested in a president of the United States of America. He shall hold his office during the term of four years, and together with the vice-president, chosen for the same term, be elected as follows:

Each State shall appoint in such manner as the legislature thereof may direct, a number of electors, equal to the whole number of senators and representatives to which the state may be entitled in the congress; but no senator or representative, or person holding an office of trust or profit under the United States, shall be appointed an elector.

The electors shall meet in their respective States and vote by ballot for two persons, of whom one at least shall not be an inhabitant of the same State with themselves. And they shall make a list of all the persons voted for, and of the number of votes for each; which list they shall sign and certify, and transmit sealed to the seat of the government of the United States, directed to the president of the senate. The president of the senate shall in the presence of the senate and house of representatives, open all the certificates, and the votes shall then be counted. The person having the greatest number of votes shall be president, if such number be a majority of the whole number of electors appointed; and if there be more than one who have such majority, and have an equal number of votes, then the house of representatives shall immediately choose by ballot one of them for president; and if no person have a majority, then from the five highest on the list, the said house shall, in like manner, choose the president. But in choosing the president, the votes shall be taken by States, the representation from each State having one vote: a quorum for this purpose shall consist of a member or members from two-thirds of the States, and a majority of all the States shall be necessary to a choice. In every case, after the choice of the president, the person having the greatest number of votes of the electors, shall be the vice-president. But if there should remain two or more who have equal votes, the senate shall choose from them by ballot, the vice-president.

The congress may determine the time of choosing the electors, and the day on which they shall give their votes; which day shall be the same throughout the United States.

No person, except a natural born citizen, or a citizen of the United States, at the time of the adoption of this constitution, shall be eligible to the office of president; neither shall any person be eligible to that office, who shall not have attained the age of 35 and been 14 years a resident within the United States.

In case of the removal of the president from office, or of his death, resignation, or inability to discharge the powers and duties of the said office, the same shall devolve on the vice-president, and the congress may by law, provide for the case of removal, death, resignation, or inability, both of the president and vice president, declaring what officer shall then act as president, and such officer shall act accordingly, until the disability be removed or a president shall be elected.

The president shall, at stated times, receive for his services, a compensation which shall neither be increased or diminished during the period for which he shall have been elected, and he shall not receive within that period any other emolument from the United States, or any of them.

Before he enters on the execution of his office he shall take the following oath or affirmation:

"I do solemnly swear (or affirm) that I will faithfully execute the office of President of the United States, and will, to the best of my ability, preserve, protect, and defend the constitution of the United States."

Sec. 2. The president shall be commander in chief of the army of the United States, and of the militia of the several states when called into the actual service of the United States; he may require the opinion in writing, of the principal officer in each of the executive departments, upon any subject relating to the duties of their respective offices; and he shall have power to grant reprieves and pardons for offences against the United States, except in cases of impeachment.

He shall have power by and with the advice and consent of the senate, to make treaties, provided two-thirds of the senators present concur; and he shall nominate, and by and with the advice and consent of the senate, shall appoint ambassadors, other public ministers and consuls, judges of the supreme court, and all other officers of the United States, whose appointments are not herein otherwise provided for, and which shall be established by law: But the congress may, by law, vest the appointment of such inferior officers as they think proper, in the president alone, in the courts of law, or in the heads of departments.

The President shall have power to fill up all vacancies that may happen during the recess of the senate, by granting commissions which shall expire at the end of the next session.

Sec. 3. He shall, from time to time, give to the congress information of the state of the Union, and recommend to their consideration, such measures as he shall judge necessary and expedient; he may, on extraordinary occasions, convene both houses, or either of them, and in case of disagreement between them, with respect to the time of adjournment, he may adjourn them to such time as he shall think proper; he shall receive ambassadors and other public ministers; he shall take care that the laws be faithfully executed, and shall commission all the officers of the United States.

Sec. 4. The president, vice-president and all civil officers of

G 2

the United States, shall be removed from office on impeachment for, and conviction of treason, bribery, or other high crimes and misdemeanors.

Article III.

Sec. 1. The judicial power of the United States shall be vested in one supreme court, and in such inferior courts as the congress may, from time to time, ordain and establish. The judges, both of the supreme and inferior courts, shall hold their offices during good behaviour, and shall, at stated times, receive for their services, a compensation, which shall not be diminished during their continuance in office.

Sec. 2. The judicial power shall extend to all cases, in law and equity, arising under this constitution, the laws of the United States, and treaties made, or which shall be made, under their authority; to all cases affecting ambassadors, other public ministers, and consuls; to all cases of admiralty and maritime jurisdiction; to controversies to which the United States shall be a party; to controversies between two or more States; between a State and citizens of another State; between citizens of different States; between citizens of the same State, claiming lands under grants of different States, and between a State, or the citizens thereof, and foreign States, citizens or subjects.

In all cases affecting ambassadors, other public ministers and consuls, and those in which a state shall be a party, the supreme court shall have original jurisdiction. In all the other cases before mentioned, the supreme court shall have appellate jurisdiction, both as to law and fact, with such exceptions, and under such regulations, as the congress shall make.

The trial of all crimes, except in cases of impeachment, shall be by jury; and such trial shall be held in the State where the said crimes shall have been committed; but when not committed within any State, the trial shall be at such place or places, as the congress may by law have directed.

Sec. **3.** Treason against the United States, shall consist only in levying war against them, or in adhering to their enemies, giving them aid and comfort. No person shall be convicted of treason, unless on the testimony of two witnesses to the same overt act, or on confession in open court.

The congress shall have power to declare punishment of treason: but no attainder of treason shall work corruption of blood, or forfeiture, except during the life of the person attainted.

ARTICLE IV.

Sec. 1. Full faith and credit shall be given in each state to the public acts, records and judicial proceedings of every other state. And the congress may by general laws prescribe the manner in which such acts, records and proceedings shall be proved, and the effect thereof.

Sec. 2. The citizens of each State shall be entitled to all privileges and immunities of citizens in the several States.

A person charged in any State with treason, felony, or other crime, who shall flee from justice, and be found in another State, shall, on demand of the executive authority of the State from which he fled, be delivered up, to be removed to the State having jurisdiction of the crime.

No person held to service or labour in one State, under the laws thereof, escaping into another, shall in consequence of any law or regulation therein, be discharged from such service or labour, but shall be delivered up on a claim of the party to whom such service or labour may be due.

Sec. 3. New States may be admitted by the congress into the Union, but no new State shall be formed or erected within the jurisdiction of any other State; nor any State formed by the junction of two or more States, or parts of States, without the consent of the legislatures of the States concerned as well as of the congress.

The congress shall have power to dispose of and make all

needful rules and regulations respecting the territory or other property belonging to the United States; and nothing in this constitution shall be so construed as to prejudice any claims of the United States, or of any particular State.

Sec. 4. The United States shall guarantee to every State in this Union a republican form of government, and shall protect each of them against invasion; and on application of the legislature, or of the executive (when the legislature cannot be convened) against domestic violence.

Article V.

The congress, whenever two-thirds of both houses shall deem it necessary, shall propose amendments to this constitution, or, on the application of the legislature of two-thirds of the several States, shall call a convention for proposing amendments, which in either case, shall be valid to all intents and purposes, as part of this constitution, when ratified by the legislatures of three-fourths of the several States, or by conventions in three-fourths thereof, as the one or the other mode of ratification may be proposed by the congress: *Provided,* that no amendment which may be made prior to the year one thousand eight hundred and eight shall in any manner affect the first and fourth clauses in the ninth section of the first article; and that no State, without its consent, shall be deprived of its equal suffrages in the senate.

Article VI.

All debts contracted, and engagements entered into before the adoption of this constitution, shall be as valid against the United States under this constitution, as under the confederation.

This constitution, and the laws of the United States which shall be made in pursuance thereof, and all treaties made, or which shall be made, under the authority of the United States, shall be the supreme law of the land; and the judges in every

State shall be bound thereby, any thing in the constitution or laws of any State to the contrary notwithstanding.

The senators and representatives before mentioned, and the members of the several State legislatures, and all executive and judicial officers, both of the United States and of the several States, shall be bound by oath or affirmation to support this constitution; but no religious test shall ever be required as a qualification to any office or public trust under the United States.

ARTICLE VII.

The ratification of the convention of nine states, shall be sufficient for the establishment of this constitution between the states so ratifying the same.

AMENDMENTS.

ARTICLE I.

After the first enumeration required by the first article of the constitution, there shall be one representative for every thirty thousand, until the number shall amount to one hundred, after which the proportion shall be so regulated by congress, that there shall not be less than one hundred representatives nor less than one representative for every forty thousand persons, until the number of representatives shall amount to two hundred, after which the proportion shall be so regulated by congress, that there shall not be less than two hundred representatives, nor more than one representative for every fifty thousand persons.

ARTICLE II.

No law varying the compensation for the services of the senators and representatives, shall take effect, until an election of representatives shall have intervened.

ARTICLE III.

Congress shall make no law respecting an establishment of religion, or prohibiting the free exercise thereof; or abridging the freedom of speech, or of the press; or the right of the people peaceably to assemble, and to petition the government for a re-dress of grievances.

ARTICLE IV.

A well regulated militia being necessary to the security of a free State, the right of the people to keep and bear arms, shall not be infringed.

ARTICLE V.

No soldier shall in time of peace be quartered in any house without the consent of the owner, nor in time of war, but in a manner to be prescribed by law.

ARTICLE VI.

The right of the people to be secure in their persons, houses, papers and effects, against unreasonable searches and seizures, shall not be violated; and no warrants shall issue, but upon probable cause, supported by an oath or affirmation, and parti-cularly describing the place to be searched, and the persons or things to be seized.

ARTICLE VII.

No person shall be held to answer for a capital or otherwise infamous crime, unless on a presentment or indictment of a grand jury, except in cases arising in the land or naval forces, or in the militia when in actual service in time of war or public danger; nor shall any person be subject for the same offence to be twice put in jeopardy of life or limb; nor shall be compelled in any criminal case to be a witness against himself, nor be de-prived of life, liberty or property, without due process of law; nor shall private property be taken for public use without just compensation.

ARTICLE VIII.

In all criminal prosecutions the accused shall enjoy the right to a speedy and public trial, by an impartial jury of the State and district wherein the crime shall have been committed, which district shall have been previously ascertained by law, and to be informed of the nature and cause of the accusation; to be confronted with the witnesses against him, to have compulsory process for obtaining witnesses in his favour, and to have the assistance of counsel for his defence.

ARTICLE IX.

In suits at common law, where the value in controversy shall exceed twenty dollars, the right of trial by jury, shall be preserved, and no fact, tried by a jury, shall be otherwise reexamined in any court of the United States, than according to the rules of the common law.

ARTICLE X.

Excessive bail shall not be required, nor excessive fines imposed, nor cruel and unusual punishments inflicted.

ARTICLE XI.

The enumeration in the constitution, of certain rights, shall not be construed to deny or disparage others retained by the people.

ARTICLE XII.

The powers not delegated to the United States by the constitution, nor prohibited by it to the States, are reserved to the States respectively or to the people.

ARTICLE XIII.

The judicial power of the United States shall not be construed to extend to any suit in law or equity, commenced or prosecuted against one of the United States by citizens of another State, or by citizens or subjects of any foreign State.

Article XIV.

The electors shall meet in their respective States, and vote by ballot for president and vice-president, one of whom at least shall not be an inhabitant of the same State with themselves; they shall name in their ballots the person voted for as president, and in distinct ballots the person voted for as vice-president; and they shall make distinct lists of all persons voted for as president, and of all persons voted for as vice-president, and of the number of votes for each, which list they shall sign and certify, and transmit sealed to the seat of government of the United States, directed to the president of the senate; the president of the senate shall, in the presence of the senate and house of representatives, open all the certificates, and the votes shall then be counted: the person having the greatest number of votes for president shall be the president, if such number be a majority of the whole number of electors appointed; and if no person have such majority, then from the persons having the highest number, not exceeding three, on the list of those voted for as president, the house of representatives shall choose immediately, by ballot, the president. But in choosing the president, the votes shall be taken by States, the representation from each State having one vote; a quorum for this purpose shall consist of a member or members from two-thirds of the States, and a majority of all the States shall be necessary to a choice. And if the house of representatives shall not choose a president whenever the right of choice shall devolve upon them, before the fourth day of March next following, then the vice-president shall act as president, as in the case of the death or other constitutional disability of the president.

The person having the greatest number of votes as vice-president, shall be vice-president, if such number be a majority of the whole number of electors appointed; and if no person have a majority, then from the two highest numbers on the

list, the senate shall choose the vice-president: a quorum for
the purpose shall consist of two-thirds of the whole number of
senators, and a majority of the whole number shall be necessary to a choice.

But no person constitutionally ineligible to the office of president shall be eligible to that of vice-president of the United
States.

No. IV.

———

WASHINGTON'S

FAREWELL ADDRESS,

TO THE

CITIZENS OF THE UNITED STATES.

———

Friends and fellow-citizens,

The period for a new election of a citizen to administer the executive government of the United States, being not far distant, and the time actually arrived, when your thoughts must be employed in designating the person, who is to be clothed with that important trust, it appears to me proper, especially as it may conduce to a more distinct expression of the public voice, that I should now apprize you of the resolution I have formed, to decline being considered among the number of those out of whom a choice is to be made.

I beg you, at the same time, to do me the justice to be assured, that this resolution has not been taken, without a strict regard to all the considerations appertaining to the relation, which binds a dutiful citizen to his country; and that, in withdrawing the tender of service, which silence in my situation might imply, I am influenced by no diminution of zeal for your future interest; no deficiency of grateful respect for your past kindness; but am supported by a full conviction that the step is compatible with both.

The acceptance of, and continuance hitherto in the office to which your suffrages have twice called me, have been a uniform sacrifice of inclination to the opinion of duty, and to a deference for what appeared to be your desire. I constantly hoped, that it would have been much earlier in my power, consistently with motives which I was not at liberty to disregard, to return to that retirement, from which I had been reluctantly drawn. The strength of my inclination to do this, previous to the last election, had even led to the preparation of an address to declare it to you; but mature reflection on the then perplexed and critical posture of our affairs with foreign nations, and the unanimous advice of persons entitled to my confidence, impelled me to abandon the idea.

I rejoice that the state of your concerns, external as well as internal, no longer renders the pursuit of my inclinations incompatible with the sentiment of duty or propriety; and am persuaded whatever partiality may be retained for my services, that in the present circumstances of our country you will not disapprove of my determination to retire.

The impressions with which I first undertook the arduous trust, were explained on the proper occasion. In the discharge of this trust, I will only say, that I have, with good intentions, contributed towards the organization and administration of the government, the best exertions of which a very fallible judgment was capable. Not unconscious in the outset, of the inferiority of my qualifications, experience in my own eyes, perhaps still more in the eyes of others, has strengthened the motives of diffidence of myself; and every day the increasing weight of years admonishes me more and more, that the shade of retirement is as necessary to me as it will be welcome. Satisfied that if any circumstances have given peculiar value to my services, they were temporary, I have the consolation to believe, that while choice and prudence invite me to quit the political scene, patriotism does not forbid it.

In looking forward to the moment which is intended to terminate the career of my public life, my feelings do not permit me to suspend the deep acknowledgment of that debt of grati-

tude which I owe to my beloved country, for the many honours
it has conferred upon me: still more for the steadfast confidence
with which it has supported me; and for the opportunities I
have thence enjoyed of manifesting my inviolable attachment
by services faithful and persevering, though in usefulness unequal to my zeal. If benefits have resulted to our country
from these services, let it always be remembered to your praise,
and as an instructive example in our annals, that under circumstances in which the passions, agitated in every direction, were
liable to mislead, amidst appearances sometimes dubious—vi-
cissitudes of fortune, often discouraging in situations in which,
not unfrequently, want of success has countenanced the spirit
of criticism—the constancy of your support was the essential
prop of the efforts, and a guarantee of the plans by which they
were effected. Profoundly penetrated with this idea, I shall
carry it with me to my grave, as a strong incitement to unceas-
ing vows, that heaven may continue to you the choicest tokens
of its beneficence—that your union and brotherly affection may
be perpetual—that the free constitution, which is the work of
your hands, may be sacredly maintained—that its administration in every department may be stamped with wisdom and
virtue—that, in fine, the happiness of the people of these States,
under the auspices of liberty, may be made complete, by so
careful a preservation and so prudent a use of this blessing, as
will acquire to them the glory of recommending it to the applause, the affection, and adoption of every nation which is yet
a stranger to it.

Here perhaps I ought to stop. But solicitude for your welfare, which cannot end but with my life, and the apprehension
of danger natural to that solicitude, urge me, on an occasion
like the present, to offer to your solemn contemplation, and to
recommend to your frequent review, some sentiments which
are the result of much reflection, of no inconsiderable observation, and which appear to me all-important to the permanency
of your felicity as a people. These will be offered to you with
the more freedom, as you can only see in them the disinterested warnings of a parting friend, who can possibly have no per-

sonal motive to bias his counsel. Nor can I forget, as an encouragement to it, your indulgent reception of my sentiments on a former and not dissimilar occasion.

Interwoven as is the love of liberty with every ligament of your hearts, no recommendation of mine is necessary to fortify or confirm the attachment.

The unity of government which constitutes you one people, is also now dear to you. It is justly so, for it is a main pillar in the edifice of your real independence, the support of your tranquillity at home, your peace abroad; of your safety; of your prosperity; of that very liberty which you so highly prize. But as it is easy to foresee, that from different causes and from different quarters, much pains will be taken, many artifices employed, to weaken in your minds the conviction of this truth, as this is the point in your political fortress, against which the batteries of internal and external enemies will be most constantly and actively (though often covertly and insidiously) directed, it is of infinite moment that you should properly estimate the immense value of your national Union to your collective and individual happiness; that you should cherish a cordial, habitual and immoveable attachment to it; accustoming yourselves to think and speak of it as of the palladium of your political safety and prosperity, watching for its preservation with jealous anxiety; discountenancing whatever may suggest even a suspicion that it can in any event be abandoned, and indignantly frowning upon the first dawning of every attempt to alienate any portion of our country from the rest or to enfeeble the sacred ties which now link together the various parts.

For this you have every inducement of sympathy and interest. Citizens, by birth, or choice, of a common country, that country has a right to concentrate your affections. The name of American, which belongs to you in your national capacity, must always exalt the just pride of patriotism more than any appellation derived from local discriminations. With slight shades of difference you have the same religion, manners, habits and political principles. You have in a common cause fought and triumphed together; the independence and liberty

H 2

you possess are the work of joint councils, and joint efforts, of common dangers, sufferings and successes.

But these considerations, however powerfully they address themselves to your sensibility, are greatly outweighed by those which apply more immediately to your interest. Here every portion of our country finds the most commanding motives for carefully guarding and preserving the union of the whole.

The North in an unrestrained intercourse with the South, protected by the equal laws of a common government, finds in the productions of the latter, great additional resources of maritime and commercial enterprise, and precious materials of manufacturing industry. The South in the same intercourse, benefitting by the agency of the North, sees its agriculture grow, and its commerce expand. Turning partly into its own channels the seamen of the North, it finds its particular navigation invigorated—and while it contributes, in different ways, to nourish and increase the general mass of the national navigation, it looks forward to the protection of a maritime strength, to which itself is unequally adapted. The East in a like intercourse with the West, already finds, and in the progressive improvement of interior communications, by land and water, will more and more find a valuable vent for the commodities which it brings from abroad, or manufactures at home. The West derives from the East supplies requisite to its growth and comfort—and what is perhaps of still greater consequence, it must of necessity owe the secure enjoyment of indispensable outlets for its own productions to the weight, influence and the future maritime strength of the Atlantic side of the Union, directed by an indissoluble community of interest as one nation. Any other tenure by which the West can hold this essential advantage, whether derived from its own separate strength, or from an apostate and unnatural connexion with any foreign power, must be intrinsically precarious.

While then every part of our country thus feels an immediate and particular interest in Union, all the parts combined cannot fail to find in the united mass of means and efforts, greater strength, greater resource, proportionably greater security from external danger, a less frequent interruption of their peace by foreign nations; and what is of inestimable value, they must derive from Union an exemption from those broils and wars between themselves, which so frequently afflict neighbouring countries not tied together by the same government, which their own rivalships alone would be sufficient to produce, but which opposite foreign alliances, attachments and intrigues would stimulate and embitter. Hence, likewise, they will avoid the necessity of those overgrown military establishments, which under any form of government are inauspicious to liberty, and which are to be regarded as particularly hostile to republican liberty. In this sense it is, that your Union ought to be considered as a main prop of your liberty, and that the love of the one ought to endear to you the preservation of the other.

These considerations speak a persuasive language to every reflecting and virtuous mind, and exhibit the continuance of the Union as a primary object of a patriotic desire. Is there a doubt, whether a common government can embrace so large a sphere?—Let experience solve it. To listen to mere speculation in such a case were criminal. We are authorized to hope that a proper organization of the whole, with the auxiliary agency of governments for the respective subdivisions, will afford a happy issue to the experiment. 'Tis well worth a fair and full experiment. With such powerful and obvious motives to Union, affecting all parts of our country, while experiment shall not have demonstrated its impracticability, there will always be reason to distrust the patriotism of those who in any quarter may endeavour to weaken its bands.

In contemplating the causes which may disturb our Union, it occurs as matter of serious concern, that any ground should be furnished for characterizing parties by geographical discriminations—Northern and Southern, Atlantic and Western, whence designing men may endeavour to excite a belief, that there is a real difference of local interests and views. One of the expedients of party to acquire influence, within particular districts, is to misrepresent the opinions and aims of other districts. You cannot shield yourselves too much against the

jealousies and heart-burnings which spring from these misre-
presentations; they tend to render alien to each other, those
who ought to be bound together by fraternal affection. The inhabitants of our western country have lately had a useful les-
son on this head. They have seen in the negotiation by the
executive, and in the unanimous ratification by the senate, of
the treaty with Spain, and in the universal satisfaction at that
event throughout the United States, a decisive proof how un-
founded were the suspicions propagated among them, of a
policy in the general government and in the Atlantic States
unfriendly to their interests in regard to the Mississippi; they
have been witnesses to the formation of two treaties, that with
Great Britain and that with Spain, which secure to them every
thing they could desire, in respect to our foreign relations, towards confirming their prosperity. Will it not be their wisdom to rely for the preservation of these advantages on the
Union by which they were procured? Will they not henceforth
be deaf to those advisers, if such there are, who would sever
them from their brethren and connect them with aliens?

To the efficacy and permanency of your Union, a government for the whole is indispensable. No alliances, however
strict, between the parts, can be an adequate substitute; they
will inevitably experience the infractions and interruptions
which all alliances in all times have experienced—sensible of
this momentous truth, you have improved upon your first essay, by the adoption of a constitution of government better
calculated than your former for an intimate Union, and for the
efficacious management of our common concerns. This government, the offspring of your own choice, uninfluenced and un-
awed, adopted upon full investigation and mature deliberation,
completely free in its principles in the distribution of its powers,
uniting security with energy, and containing within itself a
provision for its own amendment, has a just claim to your confidence and your support. Respect for its authority, compliance with its laws, acquiescence in its measures, are duties en-
joined by the fundamental maxims of true liberty. The basis
of our political systems is the right of the people to make and

to alter their constitutions of government. But the constitution which at any time exists, until changed by an explicit and authentic act of the whole people, is sacredly obligatory upon all. The very idea of the power and the right of the people to establish government, pre-supposes the duty of every individual to obey the established government.

All obstructions to the execution of the laws, all combinations and associations, under whatever plausible character, with the real design to direct, control, counteract or awe the regular deliberation and action of the constituted authorities, are destructive of this fundamental principle, and of fatal tendency. They serve to organize faction, to give it an artificial and extraordinary force—to put in the place of the delegated will of the nation, the will of a party, often a small but artful and enterprising minority of the community, and, according to the alternate triumphs of different parties, to make the public administration the mirror of the ill-concerted and incongruous projects of faction, rather than the organ of consistent and wholesome plans digested by common councils, and modified by mutual interests.

However combinations or associations of the above description may now and then answer popular ends, they are likely in the course of time and things, to become potent engines, by which cunning, ambitious and unprincipled men will be enabled to subvert the power of the people, and to usurp for themselves the reins of government, destroying afterwards the very engines which have lifted them to unjust dominion.

Towards the preservation of your government, and the permanency of your present happy state, it is requisite, not only that you steadily discountenance irregular opposition to its acknowledged authority, but also that you resist with care the spirit of innovation upon its principles however specious the pretext. One method of assault may be to effect in the forms of the constitution, alterations which will impair the energy of the system, and thus to undermine what cannot be directly overthrown. In all the changes to which you may be invited, remember that time and habit are at least as necessary to fix

the true character of government, as of other human institutions—that experience is the surest standard, by which to test
the real tendency of the existing constitution of a country—that
facility in changes upon the credit of mere hypothesis and opinion, exposes to perpetual change, from the endless variety of
hypothesis and opinion; and remember, especially, that for the
efficient management of your common interests, in a country
so extensive as ours, a government of as much vigour as is
consistent with the perfect security of liberty, is indispensable.
Liberty itself will find in such a government, with powers
properly distributed and adjusted, its surest guardian. It is,
indeed, little else than a name, where the government is too fee-
ble to withstand the enterprises of faction, to confine each
member of the society within the limits prescribed by the laws,
and to maintain all in the secure and tranquil enjoyment of the
rights of person and property.

I have already intimated to you, the danger of parties in the
state with particular reference to the founding of them on geographical discriminations. Let me now take a more comprehensive view, and warn you in the most solemn manner against
the baneful effects of the spirit of party, generally.

This spirit, unfortunately, is inseparable from our nature,
having its root in the strongest passions of the human mind.
It exists under different shapes in all governments, more or less
stifled, controlled, or oppressed; but in those of the popular
form, it is seen in its greatest rankness and is truly their worst
enemy.

The alternate domination of one faction over another, sharp-
ened by the spirit of revenge, natural to party dissention, which
in different ages and countries has perpetrated the most horrid
enormities, is itself a frightful despotism. But this leads at
length to a more formal and permanent despotism. The disorders and miseries which result, gradually incline the minds of
men to seek security and repose in the absolute power of an individual, and sooner or later the chief of some prevailing faction more able or more fortunate than his competitors, turns

this disposition to the purposes of his own elevation, on the ruins of public liberty.

Without looking forward to an extremity of this kind (which nevertheless ought not to be entirely out of sight) the common and continual mischiefs of the spirit of party are sufficient to make it the interest and duty of a wise people to discourage and restrain it.

It serves always to distract the public councils, and enfeeble the public administration. It agitates the community with ill-founded jealousies and false alarms; kindles the animosity of one part against another; foments, occasionally, riot and insurrection. It opens the door to foreign influence and corruption, which finds a facilitated access to the government itself, through the channels of party passions. Thus the policy and the will of one country are subjected to the policy and will of another.

There is an opinion that parties in free countries are useful checks upon the administration of the government, and serve to keep alive the spirit of liberty. This, within certain limits, is probably true; and in governments of a monarchical cast, patriotism may look with indulgence, if not with favour, upon the spirit of party. But in those of the popular character, in governments purely elective, it is a spirit not to be encouraged. From their natural tendency, it is certain there will always be enough of that spirit for every salutary purpose; and there being constant danger of excess, the effort ought to be by force of public opinion, to mitigate and assuage it. It is a fire not to be quenched; it demands uniform vigilance to prevent its bursting into a flame, lest, instead of warming, it should consume.

It is important likewise that the habits of thinking in a free country, should inspire caution in those entrusted with its administration, to confine themselves within their respective constitutional spheres, avoiding in the exercise of the powers of one department, to encroach upon another:—The spirit of encroachment tends to consolidate the powers of all the departments in one, and thus to create, whatever the form of government, a real despotism. A just estimate of that love of power, and proneness to abuse it, which predominates in the human heart, is sufficient to satisfy us of the truth of this position. The necessity of reciprocal checks in the exercise of the political power, by dividing and distributing it into different depositories, and constituting each the guardian of the public weal against invasions by the others, has been evinced by experiments ancient and modern; some of them in our country, and under our own eyes. To preserve them must be as necessary as to institute them. If in the opinion of the people, the distribution or modification of the constitutional powers be in any particular wrong, let it be corrected by an amendment in the way which the constitution designates.—But let there be no change by usurpation; for though this in one instance, may be the instrument of good, it is the customary weapon by which free governments are destroyed.—The precedent must always greatly overbalance in permanent evil any partial or transient benefit which the use can at any time yield.

Of all the dispositions and habits which lead to political prosperity, religion and morality are indispensable supports. In vain would that man claim the tribute of patriotism, who would labour to subvert these great pillars of human happiness, these firmest props of the duties of men and citizens. The mere politician, equally with the pious man, ought to respect and to cherish them.—A volume could not trace all their connexions with private and public felicity. Let it simply be asked, where is the security for property, for reputation, for life, if the sense of religious obligation desert the oaths which are the instruments of investigation in courts of justice? and let us with caution indulge the supposition, that morality can be maintained without religion. Whatever may be conceded to the influence of refined education on minds of peculiar structure, reason and experience both forbid us to expect that national morality can prevail in exclusion of religious principle.

It is substantially true, that virtue or morality is a necessary spring of popular government. The rule indeed extends with more or less force to every species of free government. Who that is a sincere friend to it can look with indifference upon attempts to shake the foundation of the fabric?

Promote, then, as an object of primary importance, institutions for the general diffusion of knowledge. In proportion as the structure of a government gives force to public opinion, it is essential that public opinion should be enlightened.

As a very important source of strength and security, cherish public credit. One method of preserving it is to use it as sparingly as possible; avoiding occasions of expense by cultivating peace, but remembering also that timely disbursements to prepare for dangers, frequently prevent much greater disbursements to repel it; avoiding likewise the accumulation of debt, not only by shunning occasions of expense, but by vigorous exertions in times of peace to discharge the debts which unavoidable wars may have occasioned, not ungenerously throwing upon posterity the burthen which we ourselves ought to bear. The execution of these maxims belongs to your representatives, but it is necessary that public opinion should cooperate. To facilitate to them the performance of their duty, it is essential that you should practically bear in mind, that towards the payment of debts there must be revenue. That to have revenue there must be taxes; that no taxes can be devised which are not more or less inconvenient and unpleasant; that the intrinsic embarrassment inseparable from the selection of the proper objects (which is always a choice of difficulties) ought to be a decisive motive for a candid construction of the conduct of the government in making it, and for a spirit of acquiescence in the measures for obtaining revenue which the public exigencies may at any time dictate.

Observe good faith and justice towards all nations, cultivate peace and harmony with all;—religion and morality enjoin this conduct: and can it be that good policy does not equally enjoin it? It will be worthy of a free, enlightened, and, (at no distant period,) a great nation, to give to mankind the magnanimous and too novel example of a people always guided by an exalted justice and benevolence. Who can doubt that in the course of time and things, the fruits of such a plan would richly repay any temporary advantage which might be lost by a steady adherence to it? Can it be, that Providence has not connected the permanent felicity of a nation with virtue? The experiment at least, is recommended by every sentiment which ennobles human nature.—Alas! it is rendered impossible by its vices?

In the execution of such a plan, nothing is more essential than that permanent, inveterate antipathies against particular nations, and passionate attachments for others should be excluded: And that in the place of them just and amicable feelings towards all should be cultivated. The nation, which indulges towards another an habitual hatred, or an habitual fondness, is in some degree a slave. It is a slave to its animosity, or to its affection, either of which is sufficient to lead it astray from its duty and its interest. Antipathy in one nation against another, disposes each more readily to offer insult and injury, to lay hold of slight causes of umbrage, and to be haughty and intractable, when accidental or trifling occasions of dispute occur. Hence frequent collisions, obstinate, envenomed and bloody contests. The nation, prompted by ill will and resentment, sometimes impels to war the government, contrary to the best calculations of policy. The government sometimes participates in the national propensity, and adopts through passion what reason would reject; at other times it makes the animosity of the nation subservient to projects of hostility instigated by pride, ambition, and other sinister and pernicious motives. The peace often, sometimes perhaps the liberty of nations has been the victim. So likewise, a passionate attachment of one nation for another produces a variety of evils. Sympathy for the favourite nation, facilitating the illusion of an imaginary common interest, in cases where no real common interest exists, and infusing into one the enmities of the other, betrays the former into a participation in the quarrels and wars of the latter, without adequate inducement or justification. It leads also to concessions to the favourite nation of privileges denied to others, which is apt doubly to injure the nation making the concessions; by unnecessarily parting with what ought to have been retained, and by exciting jealousy, ill will, and a disposition to retaliate, in the parties from whom equal privileges are withheld; and it gives to ambitious, corrupted, or deluded citizens (who devote themselves to the favourite nation) facility to betray, or sacrifice the interests of their own country, without odium, sometimes even with popularity; gilding with the appearance of a virtuous sense of obligation a commendable deference for public opinion, or a laudable zeal for public good, the base or foolish compliances of ambition, corruption or infatuation.

As avenues to foreign influence in innumerable ways, such attachments are particularly alarming to the truly enlightened and independent patriot. How many opportunities do they afford to tamper with domestic factions, to practice the arts of seduction, to mislead public opinion, to influence or awe the public councils! Such an attachment of a small or weak, towards a great or powerful nation, dooms the former to be the satellite of the latter.

Against the insidious wiles of foreign influence (I conjure you to believe me, fellow citizens,) the jealousy of a free people ought to be constantly awake; since history and experience prove that foreign influence is one of the most baneful foes of republican government. But that jealousy to be useful, must be impartial; else it becomes the instrument of the very influence to be avoided, instead of a defence against it. Excessive partiality for one foreign nation, and excessive dislike of another, causes those whom they actuate to see danger only on one side, and serve to veil and even second the arts of influence on the other. Real patriots, who may resist the intrigues of the favourite, are liable to become suspected and odious, while its tools and dupes usurp the applause and confidence of the people, to surrender their interests.

The great rule of conduct for us, in regard to foreign nations, is in extending our commercial relations, to have with them as little *political* connexion as possible. So far as we have already formed engagements, let them be fulfilled with perfect good faith. Here let us stop.

Europe has a set of primary interests, which to us have no, or a very remote relation. Hence she must be engaged in frequent controversies, the causes of which are essentially foreign to our concerns. Hence, therefore, it must be unwise in us to implicate ourselves, by artificial ties, in the ordinary vicissitude of her politics, or the ordinary combinations and collisions of her friendships or enmities.

Our detached and distant situation, invites and enables us to pursue a different course. If we remain one people, under an efficient government, the period is not far off, when we may defy material injury from external annoyance: when we may take such an attitude as will cause the neutrality, we may at any time resolve upon, to be scrupulously respected; when belligerent nations, under the impossibility of making acquisitions upon us, will not lightly hazard the giving us provocations; when we may choose peace or war, as our interest, guided by justice, shall counsel.

Why forego the advantage of so peculiar a situation? Why quit our own to stand upon foreign ground? Why, by interweaving our destiny with that of any part of Europe, entangle our peace and prosperity in the toils of European ambition, rivalship, interest, humour or caprice?

'Tis our true policy to steer clear of permanent alliances, with any portion of the foreign world; so far, I mean as we are now at liberty to do it; for let me not be understood as capable of patronizing infidelity to existing engagements. I hold the maxim no less applicable to public than to private affairs, that honesty is always the best policy. I repeat it, therefore, let those engagements be observed in their genuine sense. But in my opinion, it is unnecessary, and would be unwise to extend them.

Taking care always to keep ourselves by suitable establishments, on a respectable defensive posture, we may safely trust to temporary alliances for extraordinary emergencies.

Harmony and liberal intercourse with all nations are recommended by policy, humanity and interest. But even our commercial policy should hold an unequal and impartial hand, neither seeking nor granting exclusive favours or preferences; consulting the natural course of things, diffusing and diversifying by gentle means the streams of commerce, but forcing nothing, establishing, with powers so disposed, in order to give trade a stable course, to define the rights of our merchants, and to enable the government to support them;—conventional rules of intercourse, the best that present circumstances and mutual opinion will permit, but temporary, and liable to be from time to time abandoned or varied, as experience and circumstances shall dictate, constantly keeping in view, that 'tis folly in one nation to look for disinterested favours from another; that it must pay with a portion of its independence for whatever it may accept under that character; that by such acceptance, it may place itself in the condition of having given equivalents for nominal favours, and yet of being reproached with ingratitude for not giving more. There can be no greater error than to expect or calculate upon real favours from nation to nation. 'Tis an illusion which experience must cure, which a just pride ought to discard.

In offering to you, my countrymen, these counsels of an old and affectionate friend, I dare not hope they will make the strong and lasting impression I could wish—that they will control the usual current of the passions, or prevent our nation from running the course which has hitherto marked the destiny of nations: but if I may even flatter myself, that they may be productive of some partial benefit, some occasional good, that they may now and then recur to moderate the fury of party spirit, to warn against the mischiefs of foreign intrigue, to guard against the impostures of pretended patriotism, this hope will be a full recompense for the solicitude for your welfare by which they have been dictated.

How far, in the discharge of my official duties, I have been guided by the principles which have been delineated, the public records and other evidences of my conduct must witness to you and to the world. To myself, the assurance of my own conscience is, that I have at least believed myself to be guided by them.

In relation to the still subsisting war in Europe, my proclamation of the 22d of April, 1793, is the index to my plan. Sanctioned by your approving voice, and by that of your representa-

I 2

tives in both houses of congress, the spirit of that measure has continually governed me; uninfluenced by any attempts to deter or divert me from it.

After deliberate examination, with the aid of the best lights I could obtain, I was well satisfied that our country, under all the circumstances of the case, had a right to take, and was bound in duty and interest, to take a neutral position. Having taken it, I determined, as far as should depend on me, to maintain it with moderation.

The considerations which respect the right to hold this conduct, it is not necessary on this occasion to detail. I will only observe that according to my understanding of the matter, that right, so far from being denied by any of the belligerent powers, has been virtually admitted by all.

The duty of holding a neutral conduct may be inferred without anything more, from the obligation which justice and humanity impose on every nation, in cases in which it is free to act, to maintain inviolate the relations of peace and amity towards other nations.

The inducements of interest for observing that conduct will best be referred to your own reflections and experience. With me, a predominant motive has been to endeavour to gain time to our country to settle and mature its yet recent institutions, and to progress, without interruption, to that degree of strength and consistency, which is necessary to give it, humanly speaking, the command of its own fortunes.

Though in reviewing the incidents of my administration, I am unconscious of intentional error, I am nevertheless too sensible of my defects not to think it probable that I may have committed many errors. Whatever they may be, I fervently beseech the Almighty to avert or mitigate the evils to which they may tend. I shall also carry with me the hope that my country will never cease to view them with indulgence; and that after forty-five years of my life dedicated to its service, with an upright zeal, the fault of incompetent abilities will be consigned to oblivion, as myself must soon be to the mansions of rest.

Relying on its kindness in this as in other things, and actuated by that fervent love towards it, which is so natural to a man who views in it the native soil of himself and his progenitors for several generations, I anticipate with pleasing expectations that retreat, in which I promise myself to realize, without alloy, the sweet enjoyment of partaking, in the midst of my fellow-citizens, the benign influence of good laws under a free government—the ever favourite object of my heart, and the happy reward, as I trust, of our mutual cares, labours and dangers.

GEORGE WASHINGTON.

United States, Sept. 17, 1796.

ADDENDA.

―

The reader will please to insert in page 21, immediately after the 10th line, the following paragraphs.

The president does not initiate laws; they are presented, in the form of bills, sometimes by individual members, with permission of the house in which they originate; but most generally by committees to whom the subject has been referred. There are standing committees for each of the principal subjects of legislation, as *finance, foreign affairs, the judiciary,* &c. and special committees, appointed for particular subjects. A committee of the whole house is only a preparatory mode of discussion, in which a greater latitude of debate is allowed, under the presidency of a member chosen for that purpose: after the discussion has been gone through, the speaker of the house of representatives, or the president of the senate, resumes the chair, the chairman of the committee makes his report, on which the subject is debated again in a more formal manner, and the bill or report is either adopted, amended or rejected.

But though the president does not originate laws, he is required by the constitution to give to congress from time to time, information of the state of the union, and to recommend to their consideration such measures as he may judge necessary and expedient. Thus, in 1812, he recommended to them the expediency of declaring war against Great Britain, which was followed by a declaration in the form of a law, to that effect.

And in page 28, between the 13th and 14th lines, the following paragraph is to be added.

In statutes creating new offices, congress have inserted, in several instances, a clause authorizing the president in case the appointments should not be made during their session, to make such appointments in the recess of the senate, by granting commissions which should expire at the end of their next session; otherwise the vacancies not happening during the recess, the appointments could not have been made before congress met again.

LIST OF THE CONTRIBUTORS

TO THE

PUBLICATION OF THIS WORK.

John Sergeant.

Horace Binney.

Charles Chauncey.

Joseph R. Ingersoll.

James S. Smith.

John K. Kane.

Nicholas Biddle.

John Swift.

William Rawle, jr.

Joseph P. Norris.

James Page.

John Bouvier.

Edward S. Burd.

David Paul Brown.

John Cadwalader.

J. R. Jackson.

J. R. Tyson.

Charles Ingersoll.

James C. Biddle.

H. D. Gilpin.

P. M'Call.

W. B. Reed.

C. W. Sharpless.

R. Hare, jr.

L. Hollingsworth.

George A. Graham.

John L. Newbold.

John Stille, jr.

Sidney G. Fisher.

J. G. Clarkson.

Charles Gilpin.

Daniel J. Desmond.

Joseph M. Doran.

Owen Stover.

A. H. Richards.

James Gowen.

John S. Riddle.

Caleb Cope.

Benjamin Duncan.